The Insightful Journey

Walking the High Road: An A-Z Guide

The Insightful Journey

Terry Dubroy and Jillian-Rae Picco

Copyright © 2023 Terry Dubroy and Jillian-Rae Picco.
Illustrations copyright © 2023 Abbey Laferriere.

All rights reserved. No part of this publication may be reproduced, distributed, or transmitted in any form or by any means, including photocopying, recording, or other electronic or mechanical methods, without the prior written permission of the publisher, except in the case of brief quotations embodied in reviews and other non-commercial uses permitted by copyright law.

ISBN: 978-1-7389779-2-5

First published in 2023 by Thrive: Enabling Potential.
www.enablingpotential.ca

Grow the foundation of your life through the self-reflective practices offered in *The Insightful Journey: Guided Journal*. Expanding on the tools offered in *The Insightful Journey*, the authors guide you through the High Road in a new form, enabling you to create and clarify your goals for the sake of your personal thriving. Between prompts, teachings, imagery, and space to fill with your own empowering insights, this layered journey of self-inquiry will allow you to feel more connected to yourself. Whether you choose to write in this journal while reading *The Insightful Journey*, or afterwards, you will inevitably find yourself inspired and grateful to continue living your truth.

Available at www.enablingpotential.ca

About the Authors

Terry Dubroy is a loving father, husband, adventurer, and educator. He has gathered a broad range of experience throughout his life, from creating and facilitating an innovative interdisciplinary studies program for high school students, to logging over 3000 kilometres between canoes and kayaks throughout Canada. Being a natural leader and an expressive storyteller, Terry's inspirations led him to establish *Thrive: Enabling Potential*, and to co-author *The Insightful Journey*. Each chapter within this A-Z Guide represents a teaching that Terry has been enabling individuals to practise through his educational, leadership, and mentorship pursuits for decades. With his teachings in print, his intention remains the same as it has always been: to reassure you that you have all you need to bring your dreams to reality, as the most life-affirming path is also the greatest adventure.

Jillian-Rae Picco is a prolific writer who believes that individuals thrive when living in the spirit of their authentic selves. She is a Content Architect for *Thrive: Enabling Potential* and Honours Undergraduate of English Studies, and finds herself most inspired when reflecting on and researching how individuals can become the best version of themselves. Her first published work, *Canoeing with the Seasons*, poetically explored how seasonal lessons from the natural world bring meaning to personal growth. *The Insightful Journey* is her second publication, and she is grateful to have co-written this A-Z Guide about balance and self-love with her mentor and dear friend.

Author's Note

Thank you for choosing to gather more tools for your personal success, balance, and self-love in life through reading *The Insightful Journey*. When we do our 'inner work', we become more capable of illuminating and building upon what is innately good about ourselves. This guide is a meditation: each tool, or chapter, is like a gentle nudge or prompt that you may need to actualize your capacity for change. We believe that life is a non-linear journey, much like walking through the layers of a mountain. To be able to gather what we need, we have to work through undulations – terrain is ever-changing, and there are some areas that we tend to struggle walking through more than others. Yet we are all walking towards the same 'peak': a place where we can feel that we have outgrown old patterns that no longer serve us to become a better version of ourselves.

The inspiration for writing this book has been in our hearts for many years. We have both known each other for close to a decade, and met when Terry was leading a dynamic, interdisciplinary studies program called S.O.L.E. I was a budding writer at this point in time, and shortly after he noticed my skill, we began a life-affirming mentorship and friendship. Every single chapter in this guide is a reflection of Terry's teachings that I have observed and studied throughout the years between canoe trips in the Northern Ontario wilderness, conversations when walking in the woods, and his educational endeavours in the S.O.L.E. Program. Through these experiences and more, Terry has already positively impacted the lives of countless individuals by offering them nudges towards many of the lessons explored in this guide.

    The approach that we take in this guide mirrors Terry's approach to teaching: we are not trying to suggest that we can 'fix' your problems. Instead, we are here to share the best of what we authentically know and understand about life, and invite you to take and leave what resonates with you for your own journey. What resonates – what pulls you – is invariably different between yourself and every person you meet. To benefit the most from this book, we encourage you to gently challenge yourself not to take our words at face value. We encourage you to take a reflective approach to reading: to assess which chapters, sections, even sentences speak to you, and why that is. *The Insightful Journey: Guided Journal* is additionally available on our website if you are interested in taking your reflections a step further, using prompts to actively participate while reading.

    You may have arrived here after years of being

disconnected from yourself. Or, you may have been on your self-love journey for some time, and feel that you just need a self-confidence boost in a few areas. In any case – *what are* your *truths? Where are you on* your *journey towards cultivating a greater understanding of balance and self-love?* Every time that you open a page here, these are the only focuses that matter. No one's journey is the same, and we all have different work to do, a different adventure to immerse ourselves in.

With that, we would like to welcome you to the High Road – to *your* insightful journey.

Best wishes,
Terry Dubroy
Jillian-Rae Picco

Table of Contentment

Layer One: Self-acceptance

    A | Affirmations − 2

    B | Believe − 7

    C | Change − 15

Layer Two: Taking Action

    D | Doing − 24

    E | Egolessness − 34

Layer Three: Opening to Possibility

    F | Faith in Yourself − 42

    G | Greatness − 46

    H | Happiness − 54

    I | Inspire − 61

    J | Just 'Be' − 68

Layer Four: Perceiving Life Differently

    K | Kickstart − 76

    L | Laughter − 81

    M | Miracles − 86

Layer Five: Engaging with Life Differently

    N | New to the World Everyday – 92

    O | Open to Abundance – 98

    P | Play – 104

Layer Six: Enhancing Mindfulness

    Q | Quietness – 112

    R | Reflection – 117

    S | Signs to Follow – 124

    T | The Time is Now... Breathe – 131

Layer Seven: Connecting with Meaning

    U | Ultimate Calling – 142

    V | Value – 147

    W | Withitness – 152

    X | X Marks Your Spot – 158

Layer Eight: (Un)ending

    Y | Yes to Life – 168

    Z | Zeroes Are No Longer Permitted – 173

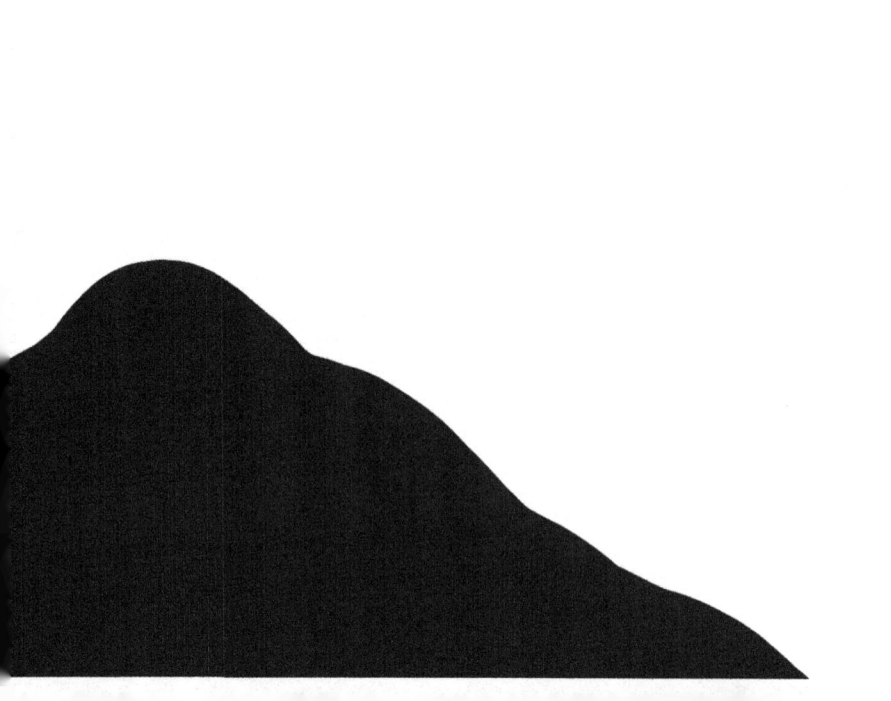

Layer One: Self-acceptance

Layer one of the High Road invites you to begin your journey by opening yourself towards greater self-acceptance and self-appreciation.

Between your flaws and complexities, your potential and strengths – we believe that in focusing more of your attention on the latter, you will become more true to the authentic version of yourself.

If you do not believe that there is much to appreciate about yourself, or that you can never change, this is a normal experience for many. We will explore how you hold all that you need within to perceive and love your many gifts.

We invite you to give yourself permission to find resonance in these pages, one letter at a time.

A
Affirmations

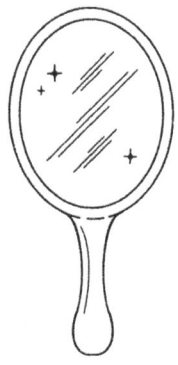

If we believe that we are worthy of living authentically in all moments that come into our lives, what might change for us? Rather than disbelieving in ourselves, we would be able to reflect all of the depth, possibility, and wonderment that exists within us. This would create a case for our higher potential, and affirm that we are deserving to live balanced, loving lives. In the moments where we feel disconnected from our authentic selves, we would know how to reassure ourselves that there is a thriving spirit within us that requires our full attention. This thriving part of us is whole – it has the capacity to fill us when we are contending with unsettling anxieties and fears. When we decide that we will only listen to our *loving* voice, rather than any unloving ones, we can become capable of echoing our own ability to take control of our lives. Through opening ourselves to affirmations, we will be able to encourage our own deservingness of our authentic selves, knowing that we are intended to thrive in life and that our potential is endless.

Affirming Your Authentic Self

While looking in an actual mirror shows your physical reflection, and all of your so-called 'imperfections', when looking within, you only need to notice the authentic version of yourself. In noticing who you are at your core, rather than looking to the world or your outer appearance for validation, you can affirm to yourself that you are already made of all that you need. Perhaps how you hold yourself back the most is through making the choice to run away from validating your authentic self, and all of the latent inner resources that you carry. You may have spent a majority of your life turned away from your inner mirror, closed off from noticing who you truly were within because what you saw did not seem to be accepted by family, friends, social groups, trends, or otherwise. As you begin your journey of self-love here on the High Road, know that fulfilment can arrive when you accept the higher version of yourself that you have been putting to the side.

When you notice that you are acting inauthentically, you can return to your inner mirror, to the conscious voice within yourself, and genuinely inquire about how you could become more loving. You can have conversations with yourself, asking why you are choosing not to love yourself by living in the guise of someone that you are not. Even when you are filled with disbelief or afraid to change, believing in who you are truly meant to be in life is the only possible route for thriving. Being attentive to how you can reflect your authenticity means looking at the parts that exist within you that need some more love, and letting yourself know that you are worthy.

What is the hidden, yet authentic version of yourself deprived of? Perhaps your heart is calling you to move your life in a different direction that is more aligned with what works best for you.

Affirming Your Long-term Thriving

Acts of self-love on the High Road need to have ripple effects – the inputs that you make need to consistently feed into your foundation, rather than serving satisfactions that you can only have for a short period of time. Short-term inputs, meaning forms of 'self-love' that feel good for the moment but deplete you beyond it, will cease your long-term growth entirely. Affirmations are not meant to be like candy, providing you a sugar rush of happiness followed by a crash back into the habits that no longer serve you. When you root your actions in the knowledge that your thriving fulfilment is a journey, and is not the same as short-term happiness, you can affirm to yourself that you are living your life in a state of growth.

Building your foundation, and reassuring yourself that you are capable of doing so, is not something that you can experience as you would going to the movies. While watching a film, you get to sit and do nothing. Afterwards, you might walk away feeling good, captivated by what you saw for some moments. Yet nearly as soon as you arrive at your car, you have likely forgotten most of the movie. It was meaningful for the moment, though ultimately nothing is of meaning unless you affirm that meaning exists within yourself. To truly love yourself, you need to look within for the truth that you would benefit from listening to before you look to the world for answers, or distractions from those answers. If you find yourself veering away from your inner mirror due to the sugar rushes of happiness that you crave in your life, now might be the time for you to reassure yourself that renting happiness is no longer effective for you. When you choose this affirmation, you can meet the desires that you know will leave you empty with self-assuring thoughts, letting yourself know how it is much more loving to build what will last. Rather than uprooting yourself from what foundationally enables your balance and contentment, instead you can look within yourself for truth, love, and deeper meanings.

B
Believe

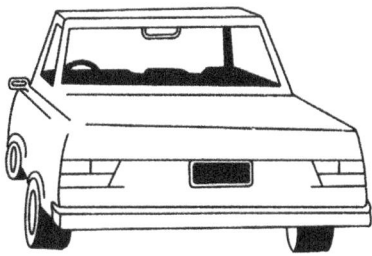

To believe is to have confidence and certainty in our truth, and our truth is this – there is an abundance of gifts for us to become attuned to within ourselves. We have the free will to be in a state of willingness and allowance for the life we have always dreamed of to unfold. We were intended for good things in this life, and trusting that they will happen is a key step in making them happen. To have trust in the abundance of what can happen in our lives, we need to reflect on which gifts within ourselves have been stored away, gathering dust. When we believe in ourselves, the perception that we have to keep all of the gifts within us tucked away in places far removed from our everyday reality can begin to change. A multitude of talents and interests exist within *every* individual – we are as deserving as anyone else for great things in life. Through learning how to own your dreams and set goals that you can believe in, not only will your self-confidence build over time, but you will also understand that you were deserving of this all along.

Getting in the Driver's Seat

Until you are ready to take ownership for the thoughts and feelings you have about yourself, it does not matter what anyone else has to say about you. It begins with *you*. The more that you believe in yourself, the closer you inch to the 'driver's seat' of your life. Now, what does that mean? In the 'car of life', your movement from the shadows of the trunk to the lightness of the driver's seat is a playful representation of the journey you undertake to believe in yourself.

Imagine being in the trunk of a car, surrounded by total darkness. This darkness represents the uncertainty experienced in adolescence, or even during the depressions of a quarter or mid-life crisis. Over time, the bumps, uncertainty, and discomfort that arise while riding in this unstable, claustrophobic space becomes exhausting. You realise that there must be more to your life than this. Once you make this discovery, you can bust your way out from the trunk, and land in the back seat.

In the back seat of the car, you can now breathe in the sight of light flowing through the car windows, bask in the feel of a smoother ride, and hear sounds more clear than the redundant echoes of the trunk. Newfound comfort and confidence can emerge. It will be easier for you to be a part of the world instead of feeling separated from it, for there is far more space in this area of the car than there was when the trunk closed you off from your life. In time, you will notice yourself outgrowing the need to remain in the back seat. Although being a participant has its perks, your longing for fulfilment will call you to take greater ownership for your vehicle's direction. At this point in your life, you can take a deep breath again, then kindly give yourself permission to crawl to the front passenger seat.

The front passenger seat will liberate you; it is so much closer to where you want to be. Along with this new freedom, you will also have more responsibility for where you want your life to go. Since the role of the front passenger is to be the navigator, arriving here will give you the opportunity to practise your gifts, and gather the confidence that you need to fully drive your life. It does take time to learn here, though what you will learn is to become patient, attentive, and present. Although you will not quite yet be your own leader, you certainly will not be a passive follower. You have a crucial role as an assistant – the drive would not be nearly as steady without your efforts.

When you have become self-assured in the passenger's seat, you will know when it is time to feel your hands on the steering wheel. Having gotten to know yourself through the car of life over time, you will be curious to know what it can be like to *fully* exist in relationship with yourself and your surroundings. In entering the driver's seat, you can celebrate that you have consciously taken the steps necessary to have greater autonomy in your life, and can enjoy the broadening views of your horizons. Then, when you are ready, you can invite those into your car that you most want to travel with. What you surround yourself with will no longer occur by chance or fate – it will occur as a result of the decisions that you trusted yourself to choose.

Setting Goals You Can Believe In

You may not have realised it, though the process of getting out of the trunk and into the driver's seat required you to dream. In pondering the story of your forward movement, the dreams that enter your mind set up guidelines for your goals. Dream achievement *is* goal achievement. While some may say it is cliche to live our dreams, if we were not living them, what would we be living? Perhaps something much closer to the stifling, isolated darkness of the trunk. There are three different types of goals, or dreams, that you can set to get yourself from the trunk to the driver's seat.

Short-term goals are measurable and realistic. When you choose these, you will want to focus on daily or weekly actions that recalibrate your mind, body, and spirit. Sometimes, we may hold ourselves back from setting goals because they seem intimidating or too difficult to achieve, though the point of these small goals is to enjoy a smooth cruise. Crashing is not possible with short-term goals, as they are low-risk: you have nothing to lose, only a small, simple task to fulfil. For instance, if you have been struggling with thinking negatively about yourself, a short-term goal would be to write down one affirmation of self-love every morning. If you have felt lonely and separated from the people in your life, a short-term goal might be to offer one compliment a day to someone who crosses your path. Focus on building forward momentum in your life and boosting your self-confidence in little ways when setting these.

Mid-term goals are dreams that will take seasons of dedication to transpire. You can set them either by building on your short-term goals, your mind, body, and spirit balance, or by asking yourself if there is a different improvement or change that you want to make in your life. These improvements can take many forms, such as through social, educational, or professional endeavours. When you were reading the car of life metaphor, what visions came to mind for you as you pictured navigating life in the front passenger's seat? Your mid-term goals invite you to forecast, venture out into the world, and challenge your comfort zone by filling your time differently. As an example, if you have been too independent and want to make new friends, you may have to build upon your previous short-term goal. Rather than maintaining the goal of giving compliments to people, you will need to sacrifice some of your spare time to be social in a new place. If your grades have been average and you want to become an excellent student, you will have to trade the extra hours you spend relaxing for a few months so that you can study. Although these changes can feel intimidating, you already imagined what it would be like to make them. This means that you want to achieve your dreams, and that you *are* capable. Mid-term goals offer you a version of yourself that has levelled up in life, an ideal to work towards with patience and humility.

Your long-term goals are the great accomplishments you have always wanted to achieve. Perhaps you forgot about these dreams when you were in the darkness of the trunk, when your gifts were collecting dust around you. Your dreams in life may have been the same since you were young, or maybe they have changed as you have gotten to know what you truly want. A long-term dream is realised each time that you envision an 'end point', an ideal place marker of what *could* be. When long-term dreams arise to you, you can simply lay claim to them and let them rest. Your long-term visions can be kept in the back of your mind when you are working on your short and mid-term goals, which will serve to keep you motivated. Over time, you will notice how smaller goals weave into your big-picture vision – your long-term goals represent the big picture of your life as it unfolds, while your short and mid-term goals are simply the steps.

You can, and you will, eventually believe in yourself to live your dreams. The journey may not be linear, as it takes time as well as an understanding of how to get there.

Though now that you have walked this chapter fully through, you are fully equipped. Walking with your willingness and imagination into the future, there is no reason that you will not find that this journey of self-love is your own coming of age into the dream version of yourself and your life. The goals that you create and achieve are designed to reinforce your confidence, along with your trust in the truth of who you were always intended to be. When you reflect on the best way that you could love yourself in life, it is through honouring the gifts you know are worth believing in.

C
Change

When we accept change as a framework for our lives, we can find calm and meaning in knowing that it is a catalyst for growth. When we decide to change from being closed to open, as the morning unfolds with the sun, we facilitate ourselves to appreciate the journey of who we are in ways that we may not have before. The same nature of the day to open towards the light mirrors the natural part of us that wants to warm up to change rather than recoil from it. With that being said, change can be uncomfortable initially. The signal it gives us can feel like fear and cause us to resist. We need to remind ourselves that change can be *good* – we were not meant to stay the same, and accepting this truth allows us to accept more of ourselves. We can enter into greater balance in mind, body, and spirit when we gently choose not to ignore the changes we know we need to make.

Changes in Mind

When you choose to accept a framework of change to guide your life, you no longer have to cling to perceptions that do not align with the transformations that life has to offer you. So far on the High Road, you have gathered the awareness of how to affirm your highest self and believe in the dreams you set into action. Change does not mean uprooting all of the good that you have permitted of yourself – it means being aware that you can have *more* of it.

If you tend to think negatively, it will not be loving to accept your thoughts as they are. Accepting all thoughts, without deciding what needs to change, will only cause stagnation. What if you allowed your mind to be flexible, to be in a constant state of learning? If you think that you already know everything, for instance, or that you are above the knowledge of how to live a better life, you will only be resisting the loving thoughts that are already innate within you. Just as a flower would wither if it were to remain closed with the arrival of the morning sun, we need to give ourselves permission to unfold towards the bright thoughts of thriving. Muddy thoughts obscure possibilities, and do not set you up to move forward on your path. They manifest as being intrusive, harbouring, or unfriendly. If you let them remain, you will disbelieve in the very goals that you have set yourself up to believe in already. Muddy thoughts can feel safe or loving if they have become familiar to you, especially if you have learned to find comfort in negativity. You may have told yourself, *I cannot control or change my thoughts, and although they may not be good for me, I am scared to change so I accept them.* These statements are also apparent when you decide to ignore the negative thoughts that you have instead of addressing or changing them.

Negative thinking patterns simply continue to play themselves out according to what we forecast for them. Even though the thoughts that do not serve us can seem fixed at first, much like the weather, they have the capacity to change. Begin by noticing one way of thinking that you need to shift. You might think that you are not worthy of loving yourself, though by thinking that you are worthy, this could become your new truth.

Changes in Body

It will be difficult to walk the High Road in your life if you do not encourage yourself to move and give nutrition to your body, though you do not have to do so in a way that you dislike. Many people perceive that to be healthy, they have to become some sort of 'perfect' person who always eats right and is extremely physically active. The notion of this perfect person, and of a perfect body, is false. However, the notion of changing and improving how you nourish your body, with a focus on making yourself feel better energetically through small efforts, is far more possible and self-loving.

The inputs that you give your body directly affect its outputs. Rather than viewing food as something that you eat to gratify your senses on a regular basis, a healthy change would be to view food as a source of energy. You need to eat whole so that you can be whole. Similarly, you need to move your body so that you can move through life's changes, accepting them with strength, flexibility, and the ability to be present rather than drained. Remind yourself that your body is a vehicle to your success.

Changes in Spirit

When it comes to changes that can be made in your heart and spirit, you need to be open to reassuring yourself that life moves in a rhythm. The path you walk undulates, and it is important to be aware of how to remain connected to yourself through it all. When you are only focused on what life gives you, and are not being a giver to yourself or others, you will feel stuck. At your core, you will feel the most content when you give to and receive from yourself and others in a reciprocal way, moving from the heart increasingly over time.

When you focus on creating how you want to feel, you will be better able to empathise and cope with your emotions, and connect with the purposeful calling of your spirit more frequently. Both your heart and spirit need ebb and flow – when you become stuck in one way of being with them for too long, you will only become stubborn and resistant to the warmth of change. New decisions often feel like a cold splash; they do not always feel warm immediately, though to feel good in your heart you need to know the coldness is simply a signal for your awakening.

When you make the effort to look within yourself and to your surroundings with an eye for appreciation of the positive aspects of life, your heart and spirit will receive what they need to feel balanced. If not, you will find yourself continually being interrupted by obstacles on your path that do not allow for your forward movement. When you look too far downward at the world's problems, or even too far up into the sky at the world's fantasies, it is more likely that you will fall over spirit-tripping roots and into emotional undertows. Keeping in mind small adjustments that you can make in your mind, body, and spirit to stay balanced in life will often surprise you for the better. Sometimes, even something as simple as considering a new perspective, making a home-cooked meal, or listening to your heart is all that you need to feel level again.

Layer Two: Taking Action

Layer two of the High Road invites you to reflect on how you can choose balanced, intentional actions in your life.

This layer specifically focuses on how being intentional with what you do in your life will solidify your foundation.

We begin to traverse into the realm of egolessness, looking at how we can take off the weight that may hold us back from moving forward at times.

D
Doing

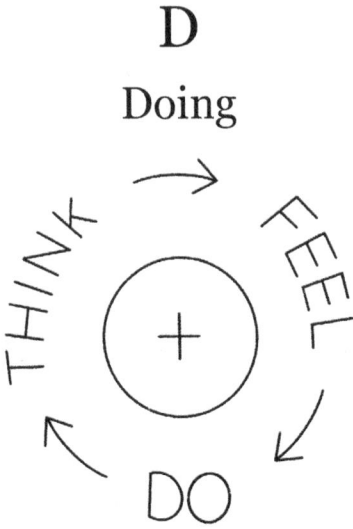

When Terry was young, an important mentor of his, Les Gorman, loved talking, writing, drawing and sometimes singing about how personal leadership worked. Through drawing something similar to the illustration above, he taught that thinking, feeling, and doing are steps in a process, circular in nature, that leads us to enabling our potential. Depending on whether you consider yourself to predominantly be a thinker, a feeler, or a doer, the areas of your 'wheel' that you will need to mend are unique to you. While every individual path towards mindful actions will be different, each step that we take requires us to first think about what we would like to do, feel our way towards it, *then* take action. Through following this process, we will find ourselves learning and expanding in life in ways that permit the growth of our highest self, that our efforts allow for movement towards our authentic truth.

Thinkers and Feelers

If you are a thinker, you innately tend to spend great amounts of time in your head. Thinking is valuable because it allows you to sit with observations and insights; when you ponder, it is as though you are gathering materials for a future project. Thoughts begin to percolate as inspiration, as this is like the morning of things. Although knowledge can be acquired in thought, understanding cannot yet be had. If you remain in the thinking process for too long, the ideas or inspirations you percolate will only brew watered-down cups, losing their potency. Thoughts become sterile and even repetitive when they are not charged by anything that you have felt or experienced.

Thinking is an essential first step, though you have to continue towards feeling and doing so that you can self-actualize, breathing life into the ideas you have generated. Like plants, we have the capacity to grow forward, and in fact, we are meant to bloom. However, plants are rooted to the earth, and their growth is dependent on them remaining in one place. Our growth as humans is a bit different, as it is dependent on how much we choose to move around and explore, letting ourselves go beyond our thoughts.

In thinking, you may spend a lot of time absorbing information, such as through watching a performance, television, reading books, or listening to music. What is it about the concepts or content you consume that intrigues, pulls, or grips you? Reflecting on this will offer you hints as to how you can become a self-sustaining doer. If you love to read, for instance, a certain character may be inspiring you *to create* art. The book's setting may be inspiring a place that you want *to travel* to. Thinking is like gathering a *to-do* list.

Moving from the backseat to the front passenger's seat through the car of life is much like the transition from thinking to *feeling*. If thinking is the process of percolation, feeling is the experience of sitting in the passenger's seat, sipping from your favourite cup and soaking up the bittersweet taste. It is about beginning to immerse yourself in what you are headed towards. To feel is to be aware of the sensations that you notice within your own emotions, whether it is the case that they are being enlivened by your thoughts or by your experiences. It is about allowing yourself to be deeply affected, and slightly uncomfortable, at the midway point between thought and action. If you consider yourself to be a feeler, you might find yourself remaining on the fence, wavering with anxiety as you wonder if going forward will cause you to fall. When we refuse to move forward, absorbing and clinging like water to cloth, we will fail to put ourselves in a position where we can learn. When you are emotionally immersed and affected, the most loving thing that you can do for yourself is to let the emotion run its course, and then follow through on the concrete action you were well on your way to taking.

The Pathway of Mindful Doing

If you would consider yourself to be a doer, it is likely that you have more 'going on' than thinkers and feelers. The pathway of *mindful* doing on the High Road is the only path that promises growth in the right direction – while productivity is valuable and promises external success, thinking and feeling need to be the steps taken prior to acting. Jumping into action without having taken the steps prior to find balance within makes it a greater likelihood that you will become derailed from your purpose and emotions.

In spite of your busy nature, you may find yourself in unnecessary situations, or notice that you simply make your life more difficult than it needs to be.

Imagine yourself walking from your apartment to work each day in the heat of the summer. For the several weeks that you have been at your job, you have always taken pride in walking the shortest route between your place and work. Yet it seems like every time you go outside, workers are doing construction on the water main, obscuring your shortcut. Every day throughout the summer, you become flustered at seeing this, but you still choose to remain on the same path, walking all the way around the pylons and signs, dodging holes and large vehicles to get back on track. In remaining on this 'shortcut', you always end up walking further, and spend more time in the sun without realising it.

We take this arduous route when we are stubborn, unwilling to admit that we are being met with resistance in spite of how much time we have spent trying to make progress. If you tend to run into the same negative experiences repeatedly, it is time to ask yourself, *how many times have I done the same thing? Is it really working for me? How could I begin to seek an alternative?* Thinking about what you can do differently, rather than trudging on, will greatly benefit you in the long-term. Not only will you choose more efficient routes, though you will also enjoy the journey of finding them.

Often, the different route that we need to take is within the tip of our nose. The next time you think to take the route of resistance, perhaps you need to explore a different pathway. Until you undergo something new, how will you truly know what is best? When you seek the optimal route of least resistance, despite it taking time to discover, you will save time and energy. Perhaps you will even find greater sources of shade for your morning walks, and find yourself enjoying new scenery. You might notice a series of park benches at the crest of a hill that you can have lunch on, so now, you do not have to eat your lunch crammed in your office – there is a better place for you to be.

When you think and feel your way towards doing, the better actions that you come to take will build your self-esteem and confidence. You will know that you are capable of learning about yourself and your surroundings. The very act of aligned doing will come to yield you the necessary experiences to build your character, and character is everything. It is what we do, and the impact that our actions have on ourselves and others, that defines us. We must be mindful about our actions because the purpose of life is to love and be loved. Through making yourself slightly uncomfortable to seek an alternative route, having noticed that the same path you have been taking for many moons is not working for you, you will build layers within your character.

Comfort Zones and Learning Zones

Character is built when our actions move us from our comfort zone to learning zones. Your comfort zone can be envisioned as a small circle within a larger one – like a nest, it is a place that you can spend time in without having to make any efforts to change or expand. Learning zones can grow like the rings of a tree. They exist in the larger space surrounding your comfort zone, representing the opportunities that there are for you to become immersed in adventures with new places and people. The more that you leave your comfort zone to enter learning zones, the more you will create new familiars, set new thresholds, and expand your options for new experiences. Even by taking one small step out of your comfort zone, you show yourself what you are capable of. You create footprints, building your self-confidence and willingness to continue developing.

When you go to the edge of your comfort zone to take flight away from your nest, at first it might be unsettling to build the momentum of your wings. It only takes a few flutters for you to find yourself at greater heights in previously uncharted territories, to have your perception entirely changed. Just as it is initially undesirable to get out of the dreamy comfort of our sleeping bags, all it takes are a few steps away from our beds to level-up in our days.

The importance of immersing yourself in the learning zones of life cannot be understated, as this is where life *is*. With that being said, your comfort zone has value when you treat it as a calm harbour, a place that you retreat to to re-energize, meet your personal needs, and simply do and be what calls to you. It is a nest for dreaming and re-energizing, for plugging in your batteries so that you can ponder where you are on your journey. Fostering a positive environment in your comfort zone can be achieved through surrounding yourself with what brings you hope for your future, and hobbies or interests that pull you to the present.

Think about the changes in mind, movement, nutrition, heart, and spirit suggested in "Change". Reconnecting with these aspects of you is exactly what your comfort zone is built for. If your comfort zone is a place that has you feeling like you are in a haze in your life, perhaps causing you to self-numb or procrastinate your self-care, reflecting on how you can make it a more loving place can be helpful.

Your comfort zone is also a good place for you to be if there is something preventing you from doing what you want to be doing right now. If there is a place that you are inspired to travel to, for instance, while you may not be able to go on a whim, you can surround the inner world of your mind and heart with imagining and planning so that its possibility becomes real. Life's possibilities do not happen within our comfort zones; while it is important for us to recalibrate and recharge, we cannot grow when we only live in the ideas of our dreams.

The more that you practise mindful doing, surpassing the edge of your comfort zone into learning zones, the more that you will find yourself *going through* the experiences you need to *grow through* so that you can *become*. Many consider growth in life to be the development that occurs from youth, to adolescence, to adulthood, to becoming an elder. Why limit yourself by age? To be an adult or elder in development, to be in the place of becoming your whole self, is to have acquired the most wisdom through learned experiences. Whether you are 16 or 60, the experiences that you subject yourself to beyond your comfort zone define the extent to which you will grow. You can expand more as a 16 year old who is seeking impactful experiences than a 60 year old who has never sought them out. When your thinking, feeling, and doing are aligned, your 'wheel' will begin to spin – you will roll into the opportunities that you need to develop in order to love your life. Doing is the final step in the process, and it is also the place of new beginnings.

E
Egolessness

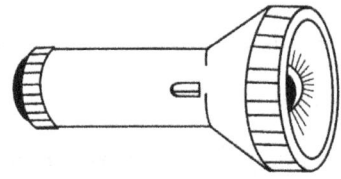

No one is more important than us, and we are no more important than anyone else. While we all have an ego, which is a basic sense of our self-esteem and self-worth, the practice of egolessness invites us to live in our ego less often. When we solely focus on our own sense of importance, we tend to repeat the same mistakes, either placing ourselves on a pedestal of superiority, or hiding underground in our inferiority. While the ego reacts to life, convincing us that we are at the centre of the universe, being egoless removes a roadblock which allows us to shed further light, to understand that we are not above or below anyone. Take a moment to reflect on the times where you have experienced your ego taking control of you in your life – have you ever allowed negative emotions to determine your actions? Have you ever pointed fingers at others rather than looking inward at yourself, or acted without considering how you impact the people around you? It is normal to have had these experiences, though choosing to behave in these ego-centred ways in the long-term does not allow us to love ourselves or others. Through understanding how to remain level in situations where your ego would otherwise restrict you, you will find meaning, and be able to illuminate your shadows.

Remembering Your Flashlight

As the sun sets after another day on the High Road, you gaze at an opening in the hill beside you, an enticing cave you feel called to explore before packing it in for the evening. On your hurried way towards the cave, you end up tripping on a rock, falling on your flashlight and breaking it. Ignoring the stinging sensation of your knees from falling, and the fact that your flashlight is broken, you continue walking towards the cave. Being too excited to care, you do not stop to consider the consequences, assuming that there will be just enough residual light from the sunset to guide your way. You enter the cave, not thinking about the consequences of having lost your flashlight, and trek on as far as you can see. Although you assured yourself that you could find your way out of anything, self-satisfaction quickly fades when darkness envelops you – you become lost. When accidents happen in our lives, and we do not stop to recollect ourselves, the ego bites off more than it can chew, often leading us to take mindless actions.

Why did you go into the cave to begin with? It is important to question ourselves when we go into the shadows of our ego. Whether jealousy, frustration, self-inflation, or self-loathing fuels you at times, you can work with these reactions by noticing when you are on the verge of entering a dark place that it is hard to return from. When you first hit your elbow and your flashlight breaks, why not give yourself a moment to acknowledge the pain, then pause and ponder your required next steps? There are always deeper truths present beyond your immediate emotional response. The ego represents our superficial reactions to life – but reflection invites us to go deeper, to think about how we can be our own source of illumination.

By simply acknowledging your flashlight is broken before acting from your ego, you honour and love yourself. You need to remember how small of a space your ego occupies compared to the vastness of the trails that you have yet to traverse, similarly to the small nest of the comfort zone and the expansiveness of flight. Is it really loving to serve your ego if all it does is hold you back?

Removing Unnecessary Weight

Your ego limits your potential. It wastes your energy jumping into holes on the High Road when you could be walking forward on your path towards your truth. When your ego is tempting you towards extreme behaviours, it does not like to hear about what you love about your life. Your ego may superficially react to others in jealousy, when in reality, you value the strengths of others. The higher version of yourself truly admires other people's stories and strives to grow as they do: it is inspiring to see others move towards their greatness. Stirring your ego by reminding yourself of what you value is useful, as having these conversations with yourself will gradually drain your ego of energy. Your ego will throw its shovel down, and pause from making things so difficult to take a well deserved rest.

The practice of egolessness can be difficult if you have become accustomed to living your life in reaction to what happens to you, rather than in the deeper state of conversation that egolessness calls you towards. You may have learned to arrive at the edge of your ego's rabbit holes not only with the intention of jumping in, though with a backpack full of stones on and no plan to get out of it, heavy as superiority or inferiority itself. The next time that you notice your ego, take one stone out and leave it at the edge before jumping in. Eventually, you will run out of stones, and you may even begin to think about some ideas for building yourself a quicker way out. When you have become efficient at escaping the trap of your ego, rather than letting your feet come to the edge, you can remember to step back, creating distance. One day, you will find yourself looking at the situation from an enriched perspective – you likely will not even want to go there anymore.

    Taking out a stone so that you can be more egoless often takes the form of changing what you surround yourself with. If there is a relationship in your life that has been adding more weight than lightness to your life, for instance, you may notice that you feel yourself bouncing off of their egoistic energy simply from being in their presence. You may need to make the difficult yet life-affirming decision to be around them less, because what we surround ourselves with is what we become. Your ego may want you to be possessive and cling to relationships, but you can remind yourself that to strengthen your own character, you cannot passively accept relationships that do not serve your higher good. Creating egolessness in your life is not about cutting things or people out mindlessly: it is about objectively assessing whether what you spend your time doing is feeding your ego, or allowing you to become a better version of yourself.

If you find your reflections pulling you away from certain relationships or experiences, it might be difficult to follow through on the truth. You might know that these individuals will react in anger or passive-aggressiveness that stems from their misconstrued sense of self. Although this may be difficult to experience, it will also affirm the decision that you made to begin with – no longer will you have to cope with, be a part of, or be shaped by these reactions in the long-term.

The understanding that you choose to have of your higher self sheds light on your ego, inviting you to have compassion for yourself and look closely at what you want and need in life. You will find yourself distracted less, surrendering to the truth of who you need to be and what you need to be surrounded by with greater frequency. Over time, and with enough conversation with the better version of yourself, you will become less accustomed to giving your ego more attention than it deserves, knowing all of the fulfilment that there is in exercising egoless self-love.

Layer Three: Opening to Possibility

Layer three of the High Road invites you to open yourself to some of the possibilities that your life journey has to offer you.

Often when we feel small or powerless as individuals, it is a direct reflection of whether we are being closed or open to new ways that we can create our own fulfilment. We will explore how you can trust yourself to experience a multitude of possibilities in your life, and fine-tune your own perception in a positive way

F
Faith in Yourself

Expanding on our discussions of comfort zones and learning zones, it is important to be aware that perfection is no longer a possibility when we are learning. When we are learning, we *must* experience our imperfections. When we are in our comfort zones, we can imagine what our ideal possibilities look like, though the moment we place ourselves in a position to learn, there will be messiness and even failure. To have faith in ourselves is to fail *forward* – to know that it is only human not to have all of the answers all of the time. Even when we are making efforts on the path to be the best version of ourselves, life has a way of reminding us that we are not God, the Creator, or the centre of the universe. When we confront our flaws, it is especially important to have faith in ourselves, to be gentle in our thoughts as we continue to move forward and learn.

Having Faith and Failing Forward

When you fail, you may want to shrink yourself away from the rest of the world. You may want to leave the expansive space of your learning zone and retreat back into your comfort zone for an extended hibernation. When we go to our comfort zone to cope with failure, surrounded by walls, our perception of the world becomes smaller, and our negative feelings become magnified. In these moments, the key you need to unlock faith in yourself is casually sitting in your pocket – you can remind yourself that you are deserving of good things in your life. There are no guarantees in life, yet trusting yourself, even when you are unsure whether you will succeed or fail, is worth it. In time, your initial efforts to find a new job will pay off, as the resumes you hand in to new places will be entirely revamped. Rather than always going to your regular safe spot for a vacation, you will finally travel to the foreign place you always dreamed about.

Often, when you have been aligning your thoughts and feelings before taking action, you will find yourself building momentum in your learning zones for quite some time before experiencing a mistake or 'failure'. Meaning that, by the time you reach a point where you could potentially become insecure from how you faltered, you can affirm to yourself that because you are on the path of making progress, you are exactly where you are meant to be. You can remember what inspired you in your comfort zone, and notice how current obstacles are offering you an opportunity to strengthen your self-trust.

Even when you are failing, this failure can only manifest as learning because you are literally walking the High Road. Although you cannot change the inevitable fact that you will encounter obstacles, you know that you are going in the best direction when you make the conscious effort not to waste your faith on the low roads. On the low roads, you wondered when you were walking on your path as to whether or not you were following the best direction. At times, you told yourself that you did not care where you ended up, and now that story is changing. Since you have chosen to have faith in yourself and in your possibilities, you can accept that while where you will end up remains unknown, you have chosen the correct journey.

When the shadows streaking the doors disturb you as you are sitting in the dark, you can stand up and see that they are being illuminated by the moon. Even with the shadows all over the doors around you, because you have stood up and made a decision with your higher potential in mind, you know exactly which door to choose. The easy doors that you walked through no longer appear as friendly – the paths they offered led you to procrastinate, question, and even lie about your truth. Now that you are interested in an abundance of possibilities, you can clearly see that while there are many openings to the low road, there is only one to the most life-affirming path – the High Road.

G
Greatness

When we give ourselves permission to have good intentions and ambitious goals in this life, we set the limits free for the potential of our authentic selves. For many of us, self-sabotage can be the most daunting aspect of our lives, and it holds us back from the greatness of our long-term vision. While greatness may sound like an impossible accomplishment, its end goal is directly connected to the steps that we choose to allow for our growth in the *now*. Reality and dreams meet at both the high peaks and within the minuscule steps of greatness, at both the macro and micro level. When we work intentionally and consistently enough towards our ideals, we will find ourselves walking the High Road for the long-term. Success, prosperity, and fulfilment are inevitable for us when we gently challenge ourselves to take a step beyond 'just-great'.

Not Settling for Just-great

Each step that you choose on a daily basis either informs you that you are moving towards a better place on your path, or that you are choosing to only go halfway. While you would have an average and relatively content life by settling for just-great, restlessness and dissatisfaction would be prominent themes in your trajectory of growth over time. Pondering subtle ways that you can take steps to turn ambitious mountains into achievable climbs will channel restlessness and dissatisfaction into fulfilment and success. In this age of endless distraction, it is all too easy to avoid taking steps beyond the bare minimum. Yet where there are the most shadows, there is the most light – the myriad of ways that you can veer away from your greatness are as abundant as the ways that you can move towards it.

To move towards greatness, you need to assess how you can shift your *perceived limitations*. Consider that any limitations that are set for yourself are, well, set *by* yourself. This means there is a choice to take a mindful step forward or mindlessly remain in the same place, because (insert excuse one here), (insert excuse two here), or even (insert excuse three here) is always yours.

One way that you can shift your perceived limitations is by being honest. There are times when your ego may convince you that you have reached a high accomplishment in life, when in reality, this perception is holding you back. You could, in reality, be more grateful, humble, and hardworking, appreciating your efforts while simultaneously imagining how much further they could go. Letting go of self-importance, as discussed in the "Egolessness" chapter, is undoubtedly intertwined with the journey of your greatness – you often have to level your ego to go further. Why decide that you have 'made it' or 'done it' when really you are constantly setting low or normal expectations, wasting more time than is necessary? If you find yourself saying that you have no energy, what if you told yourself that you could create your own energy by making a "Change"?

The Peaks of Greatness

The distant horizon, the mountain range of both future challenges and opportunities, becomes a series of daily, attainable, and achievable tasks when you encourage yourself to improve beyond your average. Each level-up for growth towards greatness can be visualised as existing in three distinct peaks.

For peak one in this mountain range, the biggest conflict in moving from just-great to greatness lies in channelling disbelief and fear into belief and trust. When you begin to make stronger decisions for yourself, you may doubt yourself or some of the decisions that you have made. When you are facing self-doubt, you can return to some of the tools you have collected on the High Road so far, and have faith in yourself to visualise what accomplishing a short-term goal related to one of your passions could look like. Peak one is the place of 'inner work', of realising that there are mundane steps that need to be taken on a daily basis to ground yourself in mind, body, and spirit. It might feel the most lonely or edgy in this phase, though you can self-affirm that these feelings are normal – you are beginning to detach from comfort and create balance. Ironically, it can feel like you are losing something big when you set this baseline, but you are only losing habits that do not serve you.

When approaching the second peak, you may find yourself satisfied at first. If you are an athlete, it is as though you have qualified for provincial championships when you wanted to make it to the Olympics; if you are an artist, it is as though you have created a great work but have no audience. Be mindful that this second peak is where many stop themselves; it is the middle, the negotiation between just-great and greatness. Your ego may return here, convincing you that you are above average, or even that you are not worthy. You may begin to settle, as you may have found belonging, made a significant accomplishment, or established a career. Resting on this ridge or continuing to tread towards your horizons is the difference between a great life and a life of greatness – you are on the edge of something that will amaze, surprise and fulfil you in ways that you *deserve* to experience. All that will be needed at this point are a couple of years (or less) of you continuing to fail forward and challenge your perceived limitations. When you find yourself having landed at self-satisfaction here, your life will continue to be inspired if you remember that there are likely only a few dark corners left to shed light on. Your opportunity at this peak will be to continue to try new things, and reassure yourself that even when you try something new and fail, this failure is building forward momentum. It is only bringing you closer to your goals, and is not holding you back.

This leads us to the fullness of peak three. At this

third peak, your long-term vision will have become clear, and you will be walking it through. Again, you may find yourself surprised – the greatness and big picture essence that you wanted remains the same, though what you are doing may be different from what you ever expected. It is this amazement that is possible to have in life that makes your greatness worth working for. Looking back from here, you will know that what you were missing at the second peak, and even especially at the first, could only have become known through your dedication to the journey.

Through every peak, notice how the same concept of mindful doing recurs – through thinking and feeling your way towards new heights of your dreams, they will only expand in ways that amaze you. Similarly to the concept of mindful doing, when navigating your way through each of these peaks, you have to think about the short, mid, and long-term goals that you have set. From this point, you have to immerse yourself in what it will feel like to achieve them, and allow that inspiration to move you forward into action. As you make progress toward your horizons, you can always return to this balanced process.

Expressing and Developing Your Originality

While some say that there are those who achieve greatness, and those who are lucky and have it thrown onto them, what defines greatness is the extent to which you express yourself in life authentically. There is no growth if you move away from your uniqueness, as greatness can only come from the spiritual nest that you have within – the birthplace of originality, the comfort zone of your thoughts and feelings that you were made to soar from. Your comfort zone of thinking and feeling is where you can find what originates from your personal wheelhouse, or niche. When you are exploring your dreams and inspirations, passively consuming ideas and perspectives will not allow you to develop our originality until you think critically about what resonates with you, and why it does.

Fear tends to creep along right before we are about to express our true selves when we never have before, or when we have only practised alone without sharing our gifts with the world. You may feel like you need to cling to who you were before when you are afraid, even though your gut feeling is that doing so would actually be more painful. You need to follow this fear, to share your differences with the world so that you can be truly seen. You are bound to either compliment something incredible that is happening in the world or create something new that changes lives. The closer that you come to natural self-expression in the fields or practices that you have devoted yourself to, the more often you may confront new opportunities that make you feel flighty or anxious – this is only because you are inching so much closer to removing your self-imposed limitations.

Beneath your limitations are the edges, lines and marks that make your mountain range so unique. Your story is yours to live. The more that you grow into yourself, trusting your capabilities with increasing conviction, you will further realise the expansive heights of your greatness.

H
Happiness

If we want happiness in our lives, we cannot chase it – though we also cannot expect that it will be achieved if we do nothing. The High Road invites us to build a long-term foundation for fulfilment in our lives, though the perception that many of us have about happiness may have actually prevented us from creating it. As we grow, it will be essential for us to change what we perceive happiness to be, and to shift our habits so that what we do parallels *thriving* happiness. Shifting our personal definition of what happiness is can be difficult to accomplish, as what many of us have learned about happiness so far comes from illusory yet widespread narratives in society and the media. A lifestyle of 'happiness', by many of the most widely used definitions, prolongs a cycle of extreme highs and lows, a repetitive game of blissful entertainment, and shifty survival.

Thriving happiness is simple, and arrives as a result of learning to change your lifestyle.

Simplicity and Happiness

Long-term, thriving happiness relates to the actions you take towards fulfilling yourself in the here and now while keeping your future self in mind. Oftentimes, choosing these actions requires you to delay your gratification. You will have to take care of your simple needs even if you would rather do something chaotic in the short-term to become satisfied. Through becoming better at nourishing yourself through mind, body, and spirit, and finding contentment in what you surround yourself with, you will be able to create your long-term happiness. Short-term pleasure is what we do when we lack the mindfulness to consider the development of our higher self. Our focus easily becomes scattered, and we do not feel whole because we are always seeking the next thrill, our next 'dose' of happiness.

Once you understand the difference between long-term happiness and temporary pleasure, you cannot fake fulfilment – not even to yourself. This is because the path to thriving happiness is simple, while pretending to be happy is complex. You know the fronts that you put on to convince either the world or yourself that you are content, and if you notice, you are often overextending into short-term pleasure rather than finding ways to be present with your journey. Always seeking out the pleasure of 'happy' thrills that cause us to wear masks might involve instances similar to trying to get a ticket for an expensive concert. A too-lengthy process of impatient moments are spent waiting in line; wads of money and time that were saved are spent away with one swipe; all for a series of moments that rapidly fade, resulting in the idea of post-concert *depression* that defines these experiences. When we surround our lives with these experiences repeatedly, this leads to a pattern where we are always thinking about the next 'happy' experience that we can have. When you invest a massive amount of time and energy into something that lasts shortly, and say that this makes you happy, maybe you need to notice that you have undertaken something quite complicated and energetically draining. Rather than thinking happiness is quick as throwing colourful confetti, you can consider that happiness truly lies in becoming a gardener, doing the hard work to make something beautiful.

  There is contentment to be experienced in simplicity

because the reality we have been given already carries the magic that we yearn to breathe in. Rather than wasting your time, energy, and money on temporary experiences so often, you can step back in your daily life and open yourself to *receiving* the simple pleasures around you. You likely miss these simple pleasures when you move too quickly or distractedly, when you are trying to reach an end point such as the close of the day. When you mindfully step back, and look at your life with an eye for what is naturally good, you will know happiness where you never did before. Too often you may be scrolling on your phone to try and find contentment, watching how exciting the lives of others seem to be, when really, the potential for your own enjoyment is already here. You can notice this potential by making the time and space to genuinely connect with yourself, to be more present in conversation with others, and to be less distracted when you are at work. Yourself, the people in your life, and the work that you do – all of these simple ingredients within your 'average' life contain happiness.

Changing What Makes You Unhappy

You cannot continue to do the same things over and

over that do not fulfil you, expecting that they might make you feel better if you press the repeat button one more time. When you open yourself to a lighter state of being, you will not become burnt out by your actions. Unhappiness tempts you to put your fingers in the flame, while contentment simply nudges you to move closer to the warmth. The kind of lightness that you create from keeping it simple, taking care of your needs, loving your life and the people within it can only inspire you to create and share more, and to seek more from within you. No longer do you have to accept patterns that cause you to fade out and feel that you are slipping into shadows and isolation. Thriving happiness invites you to open yourself to what might be a new state of being for you, where the fulfilment you experience can only be regenerated.

    When pressing the repeat button on what does not serve you, it is important to notice how you truly feel. It is helpful to practise self-awareness, to assess whether or not the repeat button is ironically working to prevent the happiness that you complain about not having. Perhaps you find yourself turning to the same coping mechanisms when you have had a rough day, and they result in you feeling worse after engaging in them than you did before. You may tell yourself that you cope this way because you are unhappy and need release, though the reality of how it truly makes you feel may not be close to good at all. By being honest with yourself, you can give your attention to what you do that causes you to feel receptive, open to having greater lightness in your mind and heart space. These ways of being may be new for you, though when you notice repetition is not serving you, why not move on? There are an abundance of new experiences that are waiting for you to press 'play'.

The Nature of Thriving Happiness

Beginning to open yourself to what thriving happiness is will allow you to understand how you can leave your repeat button behind on the low roads and continue pressing play on what matters. You may have once thought that happiness was fleeting, only arriving in short-term flutters. In reality, the High Road's satisfaction comes from building and maintaining your foundation. Only when you create chips or cracks in what you know to be solid will your lightness begin to dim. Darkness is a natural part of life, though it does not have the chance to be as permanent as the thriving happiness that you create when your toolkit is filled to the brim – and you are currently gathering tools so that this can be the case.

Thriving happiness is more permanent than you may have perceived. When you open yourself to receiving it with genuine intentions in mind (for instance, you choose fulfiling happiness because you intend to reach greatness in life), it transpires. Your choice to welcome it into your life lets the universe know that it can work in service of you, enabling you to experience less resistance when working towards your dreams. When you are not experiencing the weather of the day that you would like, what matters is finding meaning within it and being gentle with yourself. When the sun is not there, it is simply behind the clouds. If the sun were always 'out', it would actually overheat other forms of life, which would not support the well-being of anyone.

To be content in life, it simply will not be possible for us to be a positive person at all times, to always be 'out'. We burn ourselves out when we attempt this, which creates unhappiness. To experience thriving happiness consistently is to find the uplift within yourself at *most* points of the journey. Allow yourself to value what you already have and dream of how you could improve this way, rather than holding onto merely a few moments that you perceive can only make you happy.

I
Inspire

To be inspired is to be 'in-spirit', as Dr. Wayne Dyer once wrote[1]. Whether or not we consider ourselves to be 'spiritual' people, there is much truth in the fact that all human beings need inspiration to thrive. When we accept that there is a general spirit of goodness that works through the world, serving the better version of ourselves, we can learn to create clearings for this inspired energy to arrive to us. Similarly to happiness, inspiration does not come in transient, random moments – we get to cultivate it.

Loving Limits

There are bound to be times on our journey when, although try as we might, we simply feel lost, that we can no longer carry ourselves. You will probably lose your sense of

---

[1] Dyer, Wayne. *The Power of Intention*. Hay House, 2006.

'think, feel, do' balance in these instances, falling either into extreme inertia or mindless action. These are the moments where you need to remember the power that you have to create a clearing, a spaciousness that invites the spirit within you. You can generate this spaciousness by affirming that you *want* to be inspired – that you have good intentions, and need guidance to let these intentions overflow into what you are doing.

Oftentimes we develop habits that welcome toxic energy into our lives, preventing us from living more grounded and peacefully. For instance, you may have come to believe that you can only be loving if you help others carry their load, as though you are a self-sacrificing martyr. As we all have our own burdens to carry in this life, we can only be a source of support for others if we are prioritising our own growth and development first. Even if it feels selfish to believe this initially, if you are always trying to save everyone except for yourself, you will come to feel drained, rather than filled up by what you do. Knowing your 'loving limits' can allow you to make more room for inspired energy in your life. Another common example of how you might welcome draining energy into your life relates to people who always come to you for advice. If you are always making the time to care about someone who always complains, yet never seems to do any of the work they know they need to do to change, they may be polluting your clearing. In your relationships, it is important to be mindful that you cannot be a punching bag for other people's concerns, as this only enables the worst of them.

Here is a tangible way to assert your loving limits in such a scenario. When someone in your life asks you for advice for the first time, of course you can empathise and offer guidance, just as you would want that support for yourself. Even if you do not know exactly what it is that they need to hear, out of love from your heart, you can do what you are capable of with your current resources to point them in the right direction. If this person comes to you for a second time with the same unresolved issues, you can still offer them gentle guidance – though be aware that they are one step away from beginning a negative pattern. If they return for a third time, and especially many times beyond that, you know that any kindness you could offer them from your spirit is not really going to serve them, let alone you. They have the support, and they have the guidance – it is up to them to make even the smallest effort, as you cannot walk their path for them. If you continue to surround yourself with them, being their punching bag will absorb the light within you that you need to enlighten yourself and others.

Often when you are feeling uninspired and drained, this is a sign that you need to look at what you are holding the closest to you. Focus as much energy as possible on keeping yourself clear, even if that means you have to move away from something external that has become stagnant in your life.

Filling Your Place Fills You

We live at a moment in time where external successes can be acquired with or without being in-spirit, either through the trying and grinding of the ego or through the genuine flow of inspiration. The key difference between a life of spiritlessness and a life in-spirit is this – when we are working *from* ourselves, we are in a state of trying rather than a state of being. Although you can trudge ahead without inspiration, walking the High Road requires you to let the spirit work *through* you in your actions. Your ego wants you to try, while your spirit wants you to *be*. To allow yourself to be *inspired* by your work, it is important to seek even small openings in your experiences for you to be that missing puzzle piece, like the final stitch of a quilt that is missing in one corner that you have perceived. The more that you become consistent in seeking these opportunities, the more you will find yourself being pulled towards a life-giving place.

Sometimes, you may assume that looking within yourself and being introspective is what will give you the inspiration you need, yet outlets and experiences are often more fulfilling. For instance, if you have been working resiliently for some time on a creative pursuit, when the project is complete, it will be time for you to share. When you are sharing with others and your intention is to be of value to them, life comes full circle, and your spirit thrives. While we begin with ourselves first to create authentic work, inspiration is meant to be shared. The act of sharing signals to yourself and the world that you are living both an individual and collective dream, creating a more fulfiling reality for yourself and others.

In-spiritedness and Gratitude

When you feel overwhelmed and stuck in survival mode, practising gratitude can remind you of the inspiration that is already here. Having gratitude is about coming home to yourself, whether at the end of the day or within a moment, and realising that what you are sharing with yourself is sacred. Think about all that life gives to you so that you can sit with yourself at the end of the day, having been given endless opportunities to grow your strengths and unlock more of your authentic self. All of these moments are even the smallest circles of connection, like ripples in still water, that move the spirit closer to you. Your life is sacred when you allow it to work itself through, acknowledging how the betterment of yourself, of others, and your surroundings all stem from the same root – the 'circle' of life.

Even as you sleep, and your world temporarily pauses, sources of inspiration are constantly working through the world, allowing for its greater good. It is almost as though there is positive energy constantly circling through life that you can give yourself permission to tune into at any time, or better yet, to embody – when it arrives to you, this is nothing short of miraculous. When you channel your awareness into all that is working to move the world forward, and believe that it also moves you forward, you will find the inspired energy that you need arriving to you on a regular basis. You will even be able to inspire others as a result of the positive energy you have gathered, and there is hardly anything more fulfilling in life than knowing you have impacted someone's life for the better.

J
Just 'Be'

    To just 'be' is to disconnect from the hectic noise of life, and allow ourselves to connect with more natural, inherently peaceful rhythms. On our journey, we may sometimes find our path becoming a narrow plank, that our eyes are washed over with tunnel vision towards an end point. We may find ourselves trying hard to get through the days, and that we never quite feel at one with them. When we are overwhelmed or underwhelmed in our lives, we can find ourselves overextending rather than slowing down. When so much of our time is spent at battle with the external world, or even at battle with ourselves, our 'loudness dial' will be a useful tool for creating calm. Through learning how to become our own moderators when faced with the noise of life, we can attune ourselves to a harmonious state of being until it becomes our automatic mode.

Fine-tuning Your Loudness Dial

On many amplifiers and receivers, a loudness dial can be utilised to adjust the perceived noise level. Nowadays, audio engineers still distinguish between volume and loudness, emphasising that the difference between them is crucial to understanding how sound impacts us. The distinction between the two is also helpful for understanding our own personal balance. Unlike volume, loudness is how you interact with tone on a subjective level – the way in which a sound's overall feeling impacts how quiet or noisy you perceive it to be. As your perceptions are the lenses through which you view your life, noise can have a more profound impact on your sense of contentment in life than volume itself. While volume can be adjusted externally, like using the button on a remote control, you need to go inwards to self-moderate the effects of noise in your life.

Even when something in your environment has low volume, it can still be intensely loud. The prerequisite for loudness is that what happens in your life is at odds with what defines a desirable, peaceful situation for you. Although someone may not be yelling at high volume when they make a negative comment, for instance, you still do not resonate with the comment – its impact creates dissonance rather than harmony. By default, until you have fine-tuned your way to automatically supporting yourself, situations such as these will be overwhelming.

It is important to reflect on what your threshold for loudness usually is, as we all respond to stimulation differently. If your threshold for loudness is high, a roommate coming home or someone loudly closing the door in the next room may not impact you negatively, for instance, if you perceive the volume as low because these things do not startle you. If your threshold for loudness is low, in these same situations, you may become incredibly anxious. The sudden activity in your nearby environment can be debilitating after the peace and quiet that you had been immersed in during solitude. Being aware of your pattern can help you to understand whether you will more frequently need to 'dial up' from being underwhelmed, or 'dial down' from being overwhelmed.

When you are overwhelmed, slow down – realise that you do not need to exacerbate the situation any further.

You do not need to contribute to the external noise, as it is what you do to moderate your perception of noise that has potential. Before, you may have felt the need to become inauthentic in a moment like this, ramping the loudness dial all the way up within yourself to conform to the intensity of the situation. Though what you may have found was that doing so depleted your energy even further. We forget the necessity of our loudness dial when we respond to life in a way that drains us and makes us feel out of alignment with our authentic self. Yet oftentimes, all that we need to do is turn the dial down to the most subtle degree – such as responding to chaotic noise pollution by doing *nothing*. What is significant here as you fine-tune is to remember that it is an entirely internal process. Even though external loudness is the cause, it is your relationship to it, what you do with yourself to find your harmony, that matters.

When you give yourself permission to return to your noise dial consistently, you will be able to fine-tune your way towards automatically reducing noise pollution in your life. Although it does take effort to arrive at this point, making conscious efforts means that your default mode will change in the long-term – you will support yourself more frequently than you will react. Just as technology is always advancing, consistently fine-tuning our own balanced relationship with the noise of life is what will enable the process to become instinctive. All of us come with a default mode until efforts determine a new state of being. The default mode that you once had, where the noise of the external world obscured the clarity of your inner world, will shift entirely when you remember to dial it up or down accordingly.

Layer Four: Perceiving Life Differently

Layer four of the High Road invites you to believe that you can perceive your life differently, and that there is more for yourself in this life when you decide to do so.

This layer focuses on how there is more magic in the ordinary than we often realise. Rather than thinking certain aspects of your life are boring and colourless, you will gain the tools here to notice how so much has the capacity to move you into authentic self-love.

K
Kickstart

When thinking about self-love, what may come to mind for us are softer and more gentle activities, such as doing affirmations in front of a mirror in the morning, or slowing down to recharge. Yet to utilise many of the tools on the High Road mentioned so far, a strong, energetic force – a kickstart – is often needed to move into the actions of our everyday lives. Without a kickstart, our ideas can remain ideas, floating in the air around us, yet never becoming grasped and self-actualized. When walking our path in life, being resilient enough to give ourselves a jolt into action when we need it is a form of self-love. When we hide away from challenges for too long, it is often the case that we become less willing to walk our path in life;

the antidote to procrastination is effort. We need to 'do our work', so to speak, to build our willpower and experience our greatest potential.

A Kickstart for Forward Movement

To give yourself a kickstart, you will benefit from continuing to question your own preconceived notions of self-love. Only in being honest with yourself about your unhelpful habits can you create the positive changes that you need. We all experience times in our lives where we view self-love from a one-dimensional perspective, perhaps just in terms of the kind of 'positivity' that we can bask in without really having to leave our comfort zones. It is similar to the initially detrimental cycle that many teenagers experience when they first go off to college, distant from their parents' guidance for the first time. For the first few years, it is frequently the case that their lives are extremely messy – that is, until they learn to teach themselves self-discipline the hard way.

When you are struggling to recognize your potential, set goals, or even when you feel like you have completely hit rock bottom, you can think to yourself in terms of taking steps. A kickstart is the small prompt that you give yourself when you know it is time for you to take action, even though it feels difficult to begin. These prompts can take the form of asking yourself questions – what *if* you only give yourself an extra five minutes in bed when your alarm goes off, rather than keeping your eyes closed for the whole morning? What *if* you decide to go outside and get fresh air when you are feeling anxious, drained, or heavy?

As self-love is a part of what you do in your everyday experiences, and is not just a separate practice from your life, facilitating yourself to 'do your work' is a form of kindness. Some think that self-love means being selfish, letting ourselves do whatever we want. If you do not get started on your priorities as well, you will be unable to develop the resilience, strength, and self-confidence that is required to be your most fulfilled self.

There are oppositional forces that you can always be mindful of striking a balance between. Without a kickstart, you run the risk of remaining in your comfort zone, of your dreams becoming self-fulfilling prophecies. It may feel counterintuitive, but it is not destructive to think about giving yourself a kickstart. When you are weakening in your comfort zone, it is simply time to realise that a healthy step forward may just be the bitter, yet much-needed medicine you need.

Challenges as Self-love

A lot of what we have been reflecting on this guide has been challenging. It is not always easy to find higher ground in our day to day lives, to say the least. Perhaps the reason that it is so difficult to find is because we are required to tap into unknown potential within ourselves to do so. The point of giving yourself a prompt is not to place *pressure* on yourself to take action, though rather it is to give yourself *permission* to move from the heart even when it is uncomfortable. There is often no one who is harder on us than ourselves; the point of experiencing challenges is not to make our lives more difficult. The point of a needed challenge is to give yourself an opportunity to follow through on what is best for your overall well-being in that moment – the point is to honour your dreams.

It is normal to be aware of what needs to change or what needs to get done, and to stay stuck in that awareness for a time. We can talk to ourselves all day long about all of the reasons why it is important for us *to-do*, and can consciously see how it would benefit us. Remember in these moments that to strengthen your self-connection, you need to take ownership for your decisions, rather than waiting around for someone else to tell you what to do. Who else will do it for you? When it comes to your thriving, you truly do know best. Why not prompt yourself to begin?

L
Laughter

On this journey through walking the High Road, what we have continued to return to so far are some of the most simple needs in life that require our attention more consistently. Laughter is one of these needs. Through laughter, we create lightness and connection both with ourselves and others, and there is no time that we tend to need it more than when we are becoming too serious about life. Laughter can be viewed as a tenet of true happiness, and being aware of this truth is going to deepen your self-love.

A Laughing Relationship with Yourself

To laugh with yourself is to forgive yourself, appreciate yourself, and even to find some of your less-wise decisions kind of hilarious. Self-laughter is not spoken widely enough about, though it is a form of wisdom. It invites you to move on from perceiving your life as being overwhelming because of a few scrapes and follies that you experienced. Instead of waiting 'until it's gotten old', you can laugh *with* yourself, rather than *at* yourself, as close to now as possible.

There really is no reason to wait – telling yourself that you will only forgive your mistakes down the line is almost like breaking your wrist and saying, "It's just a scrape. I'll patch it up later on." As you likely know, wounds do not heal when we avoid them. It will be infinitely more healing to cultivate a laughing relationship with yourself as soon as possible, rather than having resentful wounds burrowing into your spirit – yikes! It is wonderful to think that a little giggle can prevent such pain.

Why not allow your mistakes to be what they are meant to be in your life: something that you can view as being the room for failure that you needed so that you could learn? Each time that you laugh with yourself with the intention of making light of a situation or experience where you faltered, small seeds are planted. Your mistakes are not pollutants when combined with your forgiveness and laughter, as they are what nourish you so that you can expand.

Laughter and Authentic Connection

As Lesley Lyle describes in *Laugh Your Way to Happiness*, "Research has shown that people who frequently laugh and smile are likely to enjoy a higher income, have better relationships and better health, live longer and are regarded as more attractive by others."[2] Lightening up and laughing with yourself and others will not only make your life journey more enjoyable: it will also positively impact your overall health. When you begin to notice the possibilities for laughter that there are for you in life, oftentimes, your conscience is trying to turn a moment that might have been stagnant into something that is much more authentic. At the borderline between two opposites, when laughter comes into play, people who were on the verge of a lesser version of themselves come to feel deeply through their bellies and bloom red in their faces – lasting memories are made. On a purely human level, when vulnerability and a love for the lightness recognized in others is chosen, self-control and fear of judgement can be forgotten. The spontaneity of laughter glues hearts together, knitting new bonds and rejuvenating the old.

---

[2] Lyle, Lesley. *Laugh Your Way to Happiness*. Watkins Media, 2014.

There is a deeper sense of human connection that comes through humour that you need to be willing to create and be a part of to live a balanced life. Healthy laughter shared with others illuminates and connects everyone present in a unique yet profound way. Some tools in this guide might resonate with you while they do not with others, though like music, humour is something we can all appreciate. Even those who know you best may not relate to you for your hobbies or interests, and you might find you have difficulty understanding one another. Yet the moment that laughter is brought into the picture, the seriousness of these disconnects simply does not matter. You rekindle the flames of eternal love when you step out of your mind and into your spirit, and this will often happen when you are laughing with the ones you love.

Know that genuine laughter is something that has always been valued as an essential ingredient of self-love, balance, and the human condition. You can trust this tool, even though it may make you feel vulnerable or fearful. Through laughing with others, you can experience moments that genuinely allow you to let go of all that you might normally hold onto. When something is so hilarious and you cannot stop laughing, why would you?

If you consider yourself to be more introverted or shy, you might struggle with the idea of being truly seen by others in this different gear unless you have come to trust them over time. This is because it is more natural for you to be a witness rather than a participant. You may spend so much time within yourself that the raw sense of connection that laughter offers seems worlds away. If you are more extroverted or social, having a laughing relationship with *yourself* might be more difficult than laughing with others. Being aware of the area that is outside of your comfort zone is important so that you can expand in unfamiliar areas.

Ultimately, laughter recycles the stardust we are made of. When you are willing to have authentic human connections with yourself and others, you will find your dark sky is not empty. Laughing faces create stable connections in your life, like lines of constellations being drawn together.

M
Miracles

When thinking of miracles, what can often come to mind are the needle-in-the-haystack kinds, the wishes in life that can seem entirely up to the hands of fate. The running theme of chance underpins tales of lottery winners, and because of this we may think that we will merely be lucky to experience a miracle in our lives. The truth is that real miracles are abundant – we just have to train ourselves to perceive how obvious they are. Through bringing ourselves into awareness of simple miracles in our everyday experiences, we will be able to love and celebrate ourselves and the people in our lives more often.

Miracles of the Now

Oftentimes, we are so busy thinking about what we have to do next that we miss the miracles of the now. The kinds of small miracles and gifts that unfold on your path will usually not be ones that you could have expected – they are easy to find, as they are already a part of your everyday life.

It is no short of a miracle when your family is getting along, and when your relationships are running smoothly. When it is a Friday, and you feel completely exhausted from the week, and your typically grumpy office neighbour decides to bring in donuts for everyone. When the people in your life step up to their character, making efforts to bring happiness to others where normally they would not, such instances are simple miracles. To think that many of us reading this have made it through traumatic experiences in life where we had to focus on our own survival is also a miracle. The simple fact that you are stable enough to gather the tools that you need to thrive is a marvel.

Other miracles of the now can take the form of the unexpected and coincidental. You may have experienced 'random' acts of kindness – doors being held open for you by strangers, or gentle smiles coming your way during a hard day. In the distracted loudness of the city, maybe it was a small miracle when a car slowed down for you and let you cross the road. Maybe you found yourself contemplating whether or not you should call a distant family member, and right at the moment that you were thinking of them, they called you.

In looking at your everyday surroundings with an eye for life's wonders, you can affirm that all that you need to be inspired by miracles is already here. In the "Signs to Follow" chapter, we will expand further on the fact that you are being guided in this life – miracles are a part of this guidance. The simple ways that you are blessed, whether these blessings are coincidences or direct results of efforts that you have made, deserve to be celebrated.

Layer Five: Engaging with Life Differently

Layer five of the High Road invites you to open yourself to different ways that you can engage with your life.

Sometimes engaging with your life differently will mean being more playful, while other times it will call you to broaden your perceptual horizons. In being open to new ways of living that speak to you, you will come to a deeper, yet more lighthearted understanding of your authentic self.

N
New to the World Everyday

When we learn how to be new to the world everyday, we will come to know how to love ourselves through every step of the journey. Even though experiencing our life in a new way means that we have to face the unknown, or engage with our circumstances in unfamiliar ways, our internal compass can be a grounding guide. Whether you find that the idea of being new to the world calls you to be more receptive to other individuals in your life, or to choose a more adventurous route compared to your usual routine, reassure yourself that there is always more novelty in this one life you get to live. Today is not just another ordinary day. When you wake up in the morning, you get to rise with the sun! You do not have to be the same person that you were yesterday. Both your inner world and external circumstances have opened new directions for you in even the most subtle ways.

New to Yourself

As you begin anew with yourself today, you are invited to release some of the excuses that you may normally believe in. Oftentimes, you already know what it is that you want to do to become more receptive to life, the old stories you want to let go of so that new ones can be made. You may have felt directionless before, yet now you know that anytime you sense a new direction that you want to take, it is yours to have. What you once were does *not* define you today. When you feel unsteady about making different moves in the present, you can gently remind yourself that there is value in learning how to allow your future self to unfold.

Rather than accepting wherever the wind would have blown you before, with your eyes on your horizons, you get to work towards where you truly want to go. It is similar to the movement that we make in the 'car of life' from the passenger seat to the driver's seat. Choosing to ponder and actualize new directions (in the passenger's seat) provides you with a balancing point, a reason to grasp your compass and navigate your way forward (to the driver's seat).

Familiarity and the comfort that it blankets us in can disguise itself as 'true north', as the direction that we need to follow. However, remaining comfortable is only a temporary soother, and it blocks us from the possibilities that being new to our lives promises. Instead of allowing familiarity to determine the directions that you follow on your path, notice how there are endless ways that you can leave your comfort zone to experience new growth. You can make the conscious choice every single day to become invested in and look forward to the changes that you will see in yourself in the long-term. With all of this being said – remember that familiarity and comfort are not bad things when you have self-care routines, or give yourself time to recharge from the world. Comfort is important when you allow it to refresh your life on a daily basis, so long as it is a part of your life, rather than your life's true north.

New to Your Experiences

Instead of choosing to believe that you already know

everything about the experiences you are going to have, it can be beneficial for you to realise that you do not. The compass in your pocket is all that you need for security, as you can check-in intermittently to ensure you are following the direction you aimed for. When your direction is clear, anything good will unfold. While the repetitive nature of your life before may have made it seem like every day was the same, now that you have chosen to be new to yourself, you are like a traveller, carrying light. Rather than being burdened by complexity, you have simple understanding; rather than feeling like a weak victim, you know that you have the tools to work through situations with increasing strength. Not only will you come to know yourself better when you accept the unknown, though entering the unknown intentionally will also make your future more clear.

Sometimes being new to your experiences can even occur when you take a different approach to what you do everyday. What new perspectives could you choose to apply today in the same experiences? Perhaps you could give yourself the opportunity to focus less on going through the motions, and instead channel your energy into creating memories. Instead of blurring out in the background, today you may realise your need to be a more giving individual, to make a lasting impact on someone else's life.

Sometimes, we assume that the grass will be greener on the other side, that going out and seeking a new position in life will give us all of the happiness we need. Though what if today, the opportunities to create novelty in your life await you in the most average scenarios? It may be as simple as applying some of the other tools you have learned on the High Road. If the new direction you are being called towards is to be a more loving person, giving and receiving love where you never did before can happen in a fresh chapter today.

New to Your Sense of Place

Although growth can only occur when you are actively stepping out of your comfort zone into new states of being, do not worry if you currently find yourself stagnant. At the place in which you are standing in life, there is the possibility for you to stay or go, to become immersed or detached. The newness that you are capable of experiencing in your life is going to manifest at best when you decide that there are areas of your life that you have yet to explore, that you dream about, and are willing to make happen.

When you practise being new to the world consistently over time, the rawness of the changes you once made to be more content will become your new familiar. The patterns in the quilt of your life will keep developing the more that you surrender to new beginnings, for as you go beyond what you know, you gather materials for different designs. As you create changing familiars for yourself, you will continue to be called to remind yourself of the potential that there is when you engage with life – that your sense of place in the world is dynamic and ever-shifting, yet always life-affirming. Even though you do not know what is going to happen just yet, you can *trust* that it will be for the better. Today is not just another ordinary day.

O
Open to Abundance

It is self-loving to allow our mind, body, and spirit to roam towards the possibilities of an abundant life. Many people believe, for one reason or another, that they are deserving of less from life. That they do not deserve as much love, success, excitement, fulfilment, or progress as others. We may have learned to believe that there was no possibility of prospering in a healthy way. However, we were not put on earth to separate ourselves from its possibilities, to play ourselves small and believe that there is nothing for us. We were put here to exist in a reciprocal, generous relationship with the plentitude that our journey offers. In nourishing the seeds of our dreams, actively tending to them with the sunlight and water they require to come to life, they come to abundant fruition. We will find ourselves experiencing harvests of plenty throughout our lives when we make intentional efforts to bear the fruits of our goal achievement, and to dream beyond a narrow scope about what that could look like.

The Harvest Within

One of the ideas we explored in "Egolessness" – that I am no more important than you, and you are no more important than me – can aid us in understanding how we are all equally deserving of an abundant life. An abundant life is one where you do not place limits on what you can gather or experience to live your dreams; so long as they are servicing the greater good of yourself and others, you have no reason to hold yourself back. When you make efforts that reflect your desire to expand towards your goals, life will have much to yield to you in turn.

Sometimes you may hold yourself back from prospering, whether this relates to your personal balance, the places that you want to travel to, or the experiences that you want to have. In your life, there have likely been many moments where destructive narratives given to you caused you to feel guilt or shame. Sometimes we fixate on how we are contributing to the world's problems, or even worse, we fixate only on our own. This can cause us to neglect the path of least resistance, and to feel like we are in a constant battle against our lives. Abundance suggests the opposite: that we exist in a generous relationship with ourselves and our surroundings. We are whole when we know that we are living with intentions that do not place limits on our higher self.

While walking the High Road, you have been focused on building layers rather than removing them, giving your attention to the endlessness of your own self-love. In continuing to look at what you can tend to in the now, you will come to experience harvests that are celebrations of your ideal dream achievement in life. As you continue accomplishing your dreams, what you gather at every 'table' or place will be different, though there will increasingly be plenty for you to enjoy and share. Maintaining this harvest within is simply a matter of tending to what you desire, because at your core, you will never stop wanting what is best for yourself.

Creation Cycles

We can even think about abundance by broadening the scope, reflecting on how the earth itself is a balanced, life-giving place. The sky above us, and the waters beneath and surrounding us, make it so that we exist at the midpoint. The skies above us represent a celestial, ideal, even euphoric state of being, while the depths beneath the earth suggest that there is always something lingering under the surface. Your earthly existence provides you the choice to have whatever adventures you choose – so long as you are focused on striking a balance. When you focus on the abundance that occurs when you are bringing your ideals (like the beautiful sky) into the reality of hard work (like the often bitter truth), you can, and you will prosper in the environments that you are drawn towards. With that being said, abundance cannot fall into our lap by merely thinking about it; that is the first part of the process.

The abundant earth wants you to travel authentically from your heart, to sustainably create experiences that allow you to move to different places. Sometimes we believe that we need to stay in one place, yet despite this we find when we settle that we long to experience more. Oftentimes, we are only a fifteen minute walk away from wandering into a nearby forest, from finding inspiration and peace in the nighttime stars gleaming between the trees. We may only be two months away from being able to save enough money to travel to another continent where we would experience an entirely new world. There is always the opportunity for new seeds to be planted, depending on what you want to harvest – your life is about determining what you desire to do to refresh your own perspective and find inspiration. We sometimes take for granted that the most simple elements of the ecosystem, like the fish, the flora, and the fauna, all exist in changing colour palettes throughout the world. When you find yourself stuck in thinking that there is nothing for you, it can help to remind yourself that there are worlds within worlds on this planet, worlds within worlds of dreams. There are always opportunities for new creations and new beginnings.

    Just as growth and development can occur for anyone regardless of age, the same is true for abundance. It is meant to occur at any moment that you follow through on what your conscience and your heart guide you towards achieving. You are never as stuck as you perceive yourself to be, because you are the changer. We all live our lives in a linear state of growth in our bodies: being born, growing, and dying. Though within the years that encompass this greater development, we have the opportunity to be a part of many creations that we give birth to, nourish to growth, and complete.

When something is approaching its end, and you find yourself bored and restless, this is not the time to sit on the sidelines of your life, thinking that you have experienced it all. It is time to dream about abundance – why believe in lack when you know life contains multitudes?

P
Play

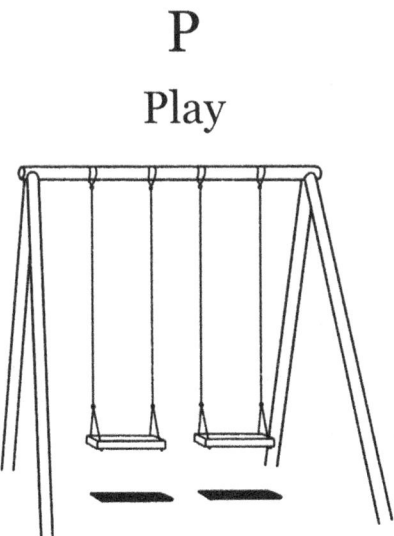

As we grow up, we are often taught to distance ourselves from what brought us joy as children so that we can become independent individuals. Yet as we grow, every part of life that we have experienced becomes a layer; forgetting about our need to play does not actually make us mature. While being an adult is often portrayed as a lifestyle of constantly putting life in order and being in a state of seriousness, more often we will benefit from tapping into our fun-loving nature. We all have a playful side, and to keep it hidden is not only unfavourable to our authentic selves, though also to the potential that we have to enjoy our lives as free spirits. By allowing yourself to be playful, there is an increased likelihood that you will make memories, build your personal self-connection, and find value in your work.

Windows for Playfulness

While playfulness may not always be on our minds, we can always make it happen. When you begin to look for windows of play in your life, you will often find that they have been waiting in the background to be discovered. Many of us grew up with the idea that in order to become a mature adult we needed to get a 'serious job' that would pay good money, even if we disliked it. That we would need to spend our lives in the same position, completing monotonous tasks, and even portraying ourselves as an authoritative, all-business figure. Yet more than anything else, it is the ego that fuels these beliefs – playfulness is egoless, as it is directly connected to our spirit.

Allowing yourself to be more playful in life will enable your authenticity, and enhance your productivity, mindfulness, and creativity. It will make you more capable of building meaningful relationships and collaborating with others. These aspects promote growth and development in ways much more profound than the egoistic notion of serious adulthood can ever offer.

Sometimes we fear being playful because we are worried about coming across as silly and immature. Yet the idea of playfulness differs from silliness – the act of play is an act of mindful doing, while silliness is mindless. When you consciously acknowledge that there is a window for play, you can immerse yourself in it for the sake of your heart and spirit. Silliness, from our perspective, more so relates to unwise acts chosen without mindful doing. Sometimes they can even be reckless or ill-intended to your well-being, but playfulness enables your growth.

Being playful can help you to realise that there is a less mechanical side to yourself and the people around you. If you notice, the adults who are thriving the most in their life tend to enjoy the journey of work as they do it, and are able to complete their duties while also knowing how to be flexible much of the time. There is no need to be rigid and upright, as there is nothing to be ashamed of, and much to look forward to, in sharing the youthful part of yourself more often. We all have an 'inner child' that wants to grow *with* us. Our self-love is at stake when we separate this part of us from our lives. We feel so much better when we let both the playful and responsible part of ourselves coexist.

Our Adult Self and Inner Child

You can also draw your inner child and adult self into harmony by making room in your regular schedule for activities that are often perceived as 'aimless'. These activities do not need to have a purpose beyond play itself. More often than not, what you will realise is that having a fun-loving experience means doing something enjoyable with someone else in your life, because play involves connection. Why not decide to make plans with someone whose company you enjoy, but you always used to put them off because you were busy doing 'adult' things?

To play is to get out of your head and into your body and heart with a childlike openness. Note that play is also dynamic and involves movement – thinking that you can satisfy your inner child with the short-term relaxation that comes through entertainment may only cut it for so long. When you were a kid, you were excited to throw your school bag on the ground and run outside, letting yourself run free. As you grow older, moving between the boxes of your home, workplace, and car, you may have forgotten how to take yourself 'out of the box' and create magical memories. Being playful is all about healing this disconnect, making the memories that will allow you to look back on your life and know that, along with working hard towards your purpose, you also had fun and enjoyed it! The world is your jungle gym, and where you choose to play on the High Road is your swing.

Playful activities do not have to be expensive, though they can be if that is what you want. If you have no idea where to begin, it can be helpful to reflect on what you used to love when you were young, whether this means getting back into what you used to enjoy, or doing something new that you are curious about. Some ideas for play include going for spontaneous adventures, making art, baking, hiking, or walking with friends. Maybe you simply need to make the decision to have no responsibilities for a day, especially if you never give yourself the time to do so. Playfulness is a state of being, rather than the act of having hobbies in your life that allow you to play. Our adult mind, for instance, may tell us that because we spent one hour making art we were being playful. Yet unless we were doing this in a way where we felt like a younger version of ourselves, letting ourselves go and not thinking about how to do things correctly, we were not in the spirit of play after all.

Notice the windows for whimsy in your life now, and

how you can fuse them with your time instead of waiting until you have children or until you have entered a certain relationship (as we often tend to think we need to do or be *something* before we can do or be *something*). Right now, at this very moment, you deserve to reconnect to the childlike energy within you. The catalyst for doing so is *you*. You can be the person to bring fun into your existing relationships, or just be a kid with yourself, for yourself. Even if you have children, rather than watching them have fun from the sidelines, why not let your guard down and join them? Every individual's version of play is going to be different, though what matters the most is that you give yourself permission. If your adult mind tries to tell you that allowing time for play means you are falling behind, affirm to yourself that you are going to return to your responsibilities feeling more energised. Your overall well-being will improve as a result of tapping into your inner child; your grown-up self grows more from letting go sometimes.

Layer Six: Enhancing Mindfulness

Layer six of the High Road invites you to expand on your capacity to practise mindfulness in life.

We create a mindful lifestyle when we notice that there are windows for us to step out of the noise of life, and give attention to the present so that we are not waiting for the day to end.

Q
Quietness

In truth, we may never find the High Road in our lives without becoming near-still in quietness. When we are feeling burnt out, making the choice to arrive at stillness refills us on a soul-level. Just as walking into a forest requires us to step off our regular path, as we settle down within ourselves we are invited to experience a different realm. There is a bridge within our comfort zones, the world of thought and feeling, that will lead us to the edge of quietness's evergreen forest. When we choose to walk the bridge and enter the forest, there is plenty of opportunity for us to experience our lives wholeheartedly – here, it is simply a different kind of life.

The Forest of Quietness

When you make room in your life to be quiet, you can think your own thoughts, feel your own feelings, and simply know what it is like to be with yourself without any expectations or distractions. It is like taking an exhale after holding your breath for so long, as there is only so much that you can handle without the shade of quietness. We literally tend to burnout without it.

You can liken quietness to a near-still forest because when you tread into nature, it is not entirely tranquil. When walking to the edge, you can often hear birdsong, wind rustling through the trees, or water trickling down a stream. It is not void of sound here, though the sounds that are present are much less over-stimulating. This is what it feels like to slow down, to begin finding presence and comfort within yourself. Before settling into quietness, you may debate whether or not you should go in. At first glance, it might seem boring or aimless to slow down – there is all of the novelty of the High Road, or even its meandering sidetracks, that you have become used to. If you consider yourself to be more extroverted in nature, it can be especially difficult to make yourself want to slow down. If you find yourself wondering whether or not you should go further into solitude, it can benefit you to reflect on the following. If you are always on the search for the next good time in life, progressing without ever pausing to steep in quieter cups, are you ever really full? Or are you just hungry?

The forest of quietness deeply fills us, and enables us to become independent rather than dependent on others. As Henry David Thoreau wrote in *Walden*, "The man who goes alone can start today; but he who travels with another must wait til that other is ready."[3] In choosing to be in solitude, you do not have to put your journey on hold, waiting to catch up with others or for others to catch up with you. Sometimes when you are busy in life, it is because you have made plans, or are looking to make plans with others. If you are constantly waiting for someone to walk with you or for something exciting to happen, at times you may need to assess if you are procrastinating what really matters: moving further into your own self-connection.

Quietness is a form of freedom, a place where you can get started on finding the trees that are best to lean your back on, or the rocks by the shoreline that are best for temporarily basking in the sun. It is *your place* that you are

---

[3] Thoreau, Henry David. *Walden*. University of Virginia, 1888.

looking for when you wander into quietness. Especially in the moments where you feel like the world has a grip on you, you need to remember that you are a small step away from returning to yourself. You can settle down in your comfort zone to recover and find stillness.

To welcome quietness into your comfort zone, ask yourself what you can do to physically and spiritually become *near*-still. Maybe you need to stay at home, in your favourite room when no one is around, with a journal and a pot of tea. Maybe you need to sit by the window in your place that has the greatest source of daylight, and make yourself a silent witness of the world. Maybe you need to put your phone on do not disturb mode, and wander along a trail in your neighbourhood at a time of day that tends not to be busy. What you do to find the forest within will change depending on what you need at the time. What matters is remembering that it is your choice to find new ways to connect with it whenever you need to.

To find quietness, give yourself permission to recalibrate. When you are beginning to drift in life, settling down can offer you a sense of buoyancy, a safe place to land. As this near-still inner world is another dimension entirely, it is one that is here to hold in place when you are beginning to feel like you are everywhere at once, and yet nowhere at all. This tool may be best for you to pull from your kit when you have been surrounded by the noise of life for too long, and especially if you feel you are forgetting the calm that comes from knowing your own voice first.

R
Reflection

When we reflect, we empower ourselves to understand where we are on our journey with greater clarity. Reflection allows us to transition a step deeper into quietness, to make space within so that we can look further into the depths of our lives. When we make the time to enter a more introspective state, observations relating to our personal truth can surface, allowing us to understand our development with greater clarity. Reflection is a place that you can visit within yourself to assess how you have been walking the High Road as of late, to notice which areas of your life you are thriving in, and which areas you are merely surviving in. It can take place the moment that you get home from a hectic day, minutes before you go to sleep, upon waking, or during any other window of time that you choose.

The Sun on the Water

In reflection, you can allow yourself to *go there* – the place within your spirit where superficiality meets depth, and what you have to trust and accept about yourself is illuminated. When you look into yourself with the intention of seeing clearly, you are choosing a higher path than muddy rumination. Rather than just looking at the intense waves of your emotions, it is as though you are looking for spaces in the water where the sun is glistening. Where the sun lingers on the water, you can see through the surface, and there is enough light for you to search a little deeper for meaning.

It is important to have an understanding of how you can make simple reflections in the present. As the here and now is the only time that you have promised in your life, reflecting in the present can allow you to have an awareness as to whether or not what you have been doing serves the higher good of yourself or others. You can think about the process of reflection like being in a conversation with yourself. For instance, when you choose an action that causes you to fall out of balance, you can inquire to yourself as to how that made you feel, and what you could do to change. In taking the time to be self-aware of how you impact others in the moment, you may notice that you are causing disharmony where you never noticed before – be on the lookout for your ego here. You may be tempted to react, but remember that this is an opportunity to learn. Maybe you never knew why some of your relationships were fragmenting until you noticed that you have a tendency to interrupt others when they express themselves to you.

Without reflecting, we often do not notice the dynamics of our day to day lives. In relatively quick, short-term reflections, it is as simple as noticing what you can do to make small pivots that support the growth of your character. In longer reflections, you can meet yourself with greater ponderance. On a weekly or even monthly basis, as an act of self-love, you can let yourself peer into the aspects of life that you do not notice when you are always moving forward. When engaging in an activity similar to the suggestions made in the "Quietness" chapter, some reflective questions you can ask related to your self-development may be, *What is going well in my life right now? What do I want to change? What am I feeling good about, and how could I allow more of this?*

Yet it is also important to let the part of you that is always concerned with growth to rest so that you can notice what you currently have in your life that you are grateful for. Which individuals in your support system are innately positive? Who cares for you and adds meaning to your life? What are the ways in which you are healthy, and surrounded by things that enable your health? Our relationships and our health are fragile – it takes effort to maintain them, yet even so they can also be easily lost in a moment. Perhaps the greatest tragedy of life, that can be prevented through reflection, is when we are not living in awareness as to how we can fully love what we have been given.

You might have an elderly family member that you want to spend more time with, though you may have been too busy, forgetting to turn down your noise dial to realise that their company is the simple joy you need. You may have become so concerned about your own problems that you have not been making time for the individuals in your life who know, understand, and love you. These truths are not always easy for us to face, and our ego may even react impulsively when we encounter a painfully honest reflection about ourselves. Still, through moving away from easy answers, you can affirm that you are making the most of your life for yourself.

The relationship that the rays and pond have

with one another, like being one another's mirrors, is the meaningful relationship that you get to have with yourself when you make the time to thoughtfully ponder your life.

Current Reflections

If you think about how a current moves through a river, much like the present moment, it is always the predominant force driving our lives. Yet the current is always changing. There are times when the river is wide, allowing the current to move more slowly; when the shape of the river is narrow, it moves at a more rapid pace. Sometimes the current even swirls back onto itself, becoming a counterproductive force in the water.

When the current is moving slowly, there is usually less risk, and greater space to process what is occurring in our lives. Reflecting during these times can allow you to practise self-awareness, to show yourself when you are being stubborn, harsh, or unloving. These reflections can take place when you are alone in a safe space, such as your comfort zone, as you ponder how you have been acting as of late in your relationships.

When the current of your life becomes fast-paced,

you may find yourself in situations where you have less control. You may find the emotional or physical well-being of yourself out of balance and in need of greater attention. While you likely do not encounter these situations frequently in your life, when you do, you need to reflect for longer so that you can make adjustments and recalibrate. You can find greater calm in these intense situations through remembering to be gentle, love yourself, and connect with your support system.

When the current is swirling back onto itself, your reflections may begin to feel counterproductive. If you find yourself beginning to overthink, overreact, or develop an extreme sense of self-importance, it is time to move away from reflection. You can realise that these reflections are not necessarily allowing you to be in the now, and as such, you can return to the present.

Life changes as consistently as flowing water. Knowing this, you need to reflect upon the transforming currents that occur in the here and now most frequently, rather than the waves of the distant past or future. With that being said, when you have more time and space to reflect in your life, without any pressure placed on you to make quick judgments, it is normal for the answers that arise to us to be all over the place. If thoughts of the past arrive to you when you are reflecting, it can be helpful to think of the idea of creating new stories as we discussed in "New to the World Everyday". Rather than repeating old stories or patterns, you could look a little deeper to notice the potential that there is for you to trust in your own courage, and begin to create the new stories you are ready for.

If you notice that you tend to escape the present by idealising a different vision for your life that has not yet manifested, do your best to return to the current. Rather than becoming concerned with an end point you foresee, instead you could think about how what you are doing in the present relates to the short, mid, and long term goals you created in the "Believe" chapter.

When you choose to reflect on your life, you can be quietly proud of yourself for choosing to give yourself perspective – for choosing to draw clarity into your life, rather than to passively accept the scattering surface. You deserve to know yourself deeply, to be in conversation with yourself so that you can own your truths. When you illuminate all that lingers beneath the surface, you become aware of your life – from this awareness, you give yourself the next steps that you need to take.

S
Signs to Follow

Road signs, or what we like to call 'meta signs', are everyday objects or circumstances in our lives that we notice carry deeper meaning when we look at them closely. Similarly to how we have street signs and maps to direct us when we are driving, meta-signs offer guidance for our spiritual path. When we are driving, signs on the road only need to be noticed through our minds and reacted to through our bodies – when we see a stop sign, we only need to think to stop and then act by pressing on the brakes. Yet all parts of our balance, our heart and soul included, need to be integrated to notice the messages that the signs to follow offer. The spiritual meaning of these signs let us know whether we are being affirmed or resisted on our path, which gives great direction for our life journey.

Meta-signs in the Natural World

Whether you are experiencing a stable or unstable period in your life, you always have the potential to notice how you are being guided. In Steve Van Matre and Bill Weiler's nature anthology, *The Earth Speaks,* the authors describe that, "Yes, the earth speaks, but only to those who can hear with their hearts."[4] This quote has been a longstanding source of inspiration for us, as the earth has a way of speaking to us through subtle yet important offerings. When you wander away from your everyday surroundings, either immersing yourself in nature or walking nearby it, you will encounter a variety of meta-signs. The earth has an authentic, sometimes even surreal way of letting us know that it understands us, and that it wants to steer us towards a higher path in our lives. To notice meta-signs, you simply need to walk outside with the intention of noticing details in your surrounding landscapes, as well as the animals that stand out to you.

When you are normally walking, you may find yourself always staring at the ground. When looking for

---

[4] Van Matre, Steve and Weiler, Bill. *The Earth Speaks*. Institute for Earth Education, 1983.

meta-signs, you can instead look towards your horizons – both literally and metaphorically. You may notice a distant hill or an interesting rock outcrop when you look up, and find that speaks to you as the patience you need to practise on your journey. As cliché as it may sound, it may be a meta-sign when you go for a walk and the sun has come out after several grey days, representing the rewards that arrive after a period of difficulty. You may hear the whisper of wind blowing through the trees, and find that this draws you into the present as a reminder to stay grounded. Maybe the presence of the trees even speak to you as a holistic change that you want to make in your lifestyle, such as connecting with nature more often. It is important to know what resonates with you in your own life, as all animals and living things have a multitude of meanings.

When you are looking towards something being over, rather than being fully present, you are more likely to miss the presence of spiritual encounters. Meta-signs can only make an appearance if you are doing the mindful work to receive them, as they can only reach you when you begin to take off blinders in your mind. Through making the effort to walk in your surroundings intentionally, no longer looking at the world with tunnel vision, you will become receptive to what you would normally miss.

If you have been working on yourself spiritually for some time, and still feel like you are not receiving guidance in your life, it can help to be aware of what you are more apt to notice and more likely to overlook. Are you more likely to follow the larger signs, the ones that appear to you boldly, while smaller, subtle details pass you by? Perhaps you have a tendency to obsess over small details, looking too closely at what you think one sign is to acknowledge that there are potentially many others. If you are more prone to look for what stands out immediately, you might go into nature looking for large mammals like deer, bears, and the like to find meaning. Rather than becoming flustered when you do not see anything 'out of the ordinary', the sign that may be calling you is miniscule, something that you may even normally disregard. Butterflies, dragonflies, moths, or animal footprints in the snow are meta-signs; just as woodpeckers blending into the wood of streetlights, or ladybugs clinging to ferns can be.

In *Ojibway Clans: Animal Totems and Clans*, Ojibway author and illustrator Mark Anthony Jacobson describes and depicts the clan system of the Ojibway First Nations people of Canada. Jacobson writes, "The animal totems help us identify the different responsibilities each clan has in supporting and leading the community. We associate special gifts with each animal totem".[5] For instance, the gifts that turtles embody are healing, a change of heart, love, care, and wise decision making. Loons represent the art of sharing, the freedom to be yourself, beauty of spirit, and peacemaking. A porcupine signifies warrior strength through the ability to be responsible, defend, protect, and ask for help. Deer indicate kindheartedness, agility, healthiness, vision, and being the best that you can be. A butterfly symbolises transformation, understanding others and yourself, and being thankful for change. All of these animals can appear in your life as potential signs to follow, and this is simply the tip of the iceberg when it comes to animals and their spiritual meaning.

When Resistance is Guidance

What happens in our lives externally is often a mirror image of what we are feeling internally. When things are going well for you, this truth is peaceful, as the meta-signs

---

[5] Jacobson, Mark Anthony. *Ojibway Clans: Animal Totems and Spirits*. Native Northwest, 2015.

that you see will affirm your journey. However, when you are struggling internally, you may be prone to avoiding signs of resistance on your path. Whether in your personal relationships or greater life circumstances, it can be painful to feel like you are being resisted, especially when you have been diligently (or perhaps even stubbornly) making efforts over time. There comes a point where you need to admit when you are losing your energy, making things harder for yourself than they need to be by remaining in a situation that no longer serves you. Remember: the universe is *for* you, not against you. Life wants you to win, though how it expresses this fact is by reflecting the truth, which is often painful. It is much more painful, however, to avoid these signs over time. Signs of resistance are a form of guidance – it is not always what you will want to accept, though it is what you need so that you can transform.

Signs of resistance offer a path for failing forward. When you have been working very hard to make something work against a growing resistance, it can feel like the universe's steel toe boots have kicked you down as you start to reconsider everything you have done. Maybe you just need to gently listen to the truth. It is okay to change paths or even to start again. Take it a day at a time, and choose to make small pivots rather than succumb to self-doubt. Why burn out where you are when you can burn brightly somewhere new? This is the life-affirming message that meta-signs invite you to receive.

T
The Time is Now... Breathe

In modern life, many of us have become accustomed to measuring time in minutes, hours, days, weeks, months, years, and so on. Currently, there is only one time – *now!* It is moment o'clock. There is no point in waiting for a time that is already here. Dedicating ourselves to accepting life as it exists in the here and now can enable us to maximize the finite resource of the time we have been given in our lives. You can begin to accept that the time is now by affirming – *I am in the right place at the right time in choosing to read this chapter*. If, when you say this, you find yourself thinking that something else is calling to your higher good, why not choose this instead? All that is guaranteed in our lives is what we have right now. Making ourselves receptive to the moment, and doing what we purposefully desire to do, will allow us to fully be where we are, rather than distant.

Trading Escapism for the Now

As great as being fully in the now may sound, the present moment often may not always come across as a place of loving opportunity. When you reach beyond the current moment, seeking to escape or drift away from what you are doing, you tend to do so out of habits that allow you to escape your own journey. You might find yourself revisiting the past and future, or even procrastinating your needs, to exist anywhere other than in the now. Maybe you have the tendency of tightly measuring time so that you can reach end goals. In these circumstances, what you need to do is *accept what is*. When we are trying to escape from a moment, we typically do so because we either do not want to be there, or because we lack the trust to simply be present with ourselves. Oddly enough, it is life-affirming to acknowledge the root, to know that there is somewhere else you would rather be.

It is much easier to be present in our 'off' time from the world, though if we are only present when we are off-duty, opportunities to find balance, grow, and love ourselves will be missed. The feeling that you have when you are engrossed in an episode, listening to music, or otherwise, can also be found when you view each moment as having the potential to open more for you in life. You may have been taught that presence was a 'present' given to you from other people, objects, or sources – that being present was not something you could ever do yourself. Just as we explored in "New to the World Everyday", there is always more to life for you to experience when you decide that you can increasingly have fulfiling moments that ground you to where you are.

      Have you ever experienced the feeling that you are in the right place at the right time? A time where you became so at one with the moment that you were hardly thinking about anything else? If you have not, you have likely at least wanted to experience this feeling before. It is an innate need within all of us to master the present, to give ourselves permission to know that our time is a sacred resource, and does not have to be treated as otherwise. When we are present, we become aware of our own unfolding, and more capable of appreciating the forward movement that we make. Right at the moment where you are about to drift from the present, catch yourself before the fall. You can let yourself know that you are going to stay: daylight is still here. More petals have yet to unfurl. The key to fully unfurling to the present is focusing on the moment of now, in which a particular petal is unravelling itself like a chapter. A fleeting chapter that, as you witness its passing, fully blooms towards your story of the High Road, yielding to its themes of balance and self-love.

It can be overwhelming when you are so excited about life, when there is so much that you want to do, or the opposite – if the great picture of the day overwhelms you into feeling that you would rather do nothing at all. Just as the line between excitement and fear is thin, so are the lines between activity and passivity, presence and distance. All that you need to be mindful of time is to take the step that is your priority and your desire. With a solid and intentional purpose, rather than viewing your daily obligations as being things that you *have* to do, instead acknowledge that they are the path towards the peak of today.

Even if you continue to stop yourself from being present in moments where you could grow your awareness, assure yourself that this is okay. It does take time to outgrow old habits of escapism, and although your time in the future is not necessarily promised, anytime that you become aware you have the opportunity to receive the gift of the present again is a little miracle. It may be too late now, though it is not too late for the next now (which is right now, and right now, and...).

Breathe, Trust, Repeat

Breathing through moments where you are struggling to be present is a physical way that you can signal to yourself that you are here, and that there is much for you. There are many benefits to breathing for a minute, or a few if you have the time, before you begin your daily responsibilities. These mere minutes will calm your nervous system and set you up for a successful day. Breathing deeply is an affirmation that you can give to yourself in the moment when you are struggling to be present, as it will help you to soften and melt a little bit in love so that you are no longer wasting your energy on a battle within. When you slow down and breathe, much of the energy that had been working against the current moment can flow directly into it, allowing you to feel grounded and connected to yourself.

Staying focused on your breathing and remaining in the present might sound too simple to be true. But just as it feels better to love ourselves than it does to resist ourselves, it feels better to be in the moment than to reject it. When we are busy or stressed in our minds, we begin to feel disconnected from our bodies, and can often detach from our breath. This disconnection causes us to amplify how overwhelmed we feel, yet the moment we remind ourselves that we purposefully want to bridge the gap we are feeling, we have already taken the first step that will enable us to take some conscious breaths. From this point, we can intentionally find the space and time to consciously close our eyes, and surrender to our own breath. Our thoughts and feelings may still be scattered for some time, but we can anchor ourselves in our intention, and our purpose for remaining with our breath, which is so that we can return to the remainder of the day feeling centred and capable. If making the decision to breathe and surrender to the current moment feels strange and unknown to you at first, let yourself know that it only feels difficult because you have just begun. Whether consciously or subconsciously, many of us have learned to prevent ourselves from simply breathing and practising presence and to instead push through without being mindful at all. The tool of breathing, when practised either to start your day or during times when you are overwhelmed throughout it, will create a clearer, less overwhelming state of being for you.

Giving your attention to senses beyond your breath is another way in which you can fully live within moment o'clock. It is as simple as noticing your own body throughout the day, observing how the feelings that arise within you are connected to how your body is doing. On the days where you are stressed, maybe just noticing that your shoulders and face have tightened, and that you might even be grinding your teeth, can help you to accept that you need to breathe. When you feel like you are encountering a challenge, noticing how your body is strained or sore can help you to be gentle with yourself, and even to slow down as you continue. These micro-adjustments will help to prevent you from burning out, and it will often surprise you how only three to five minutes of awareness rebuilds your spirit.

The signals that you receive through your senses may engulf you if they are not what you want to experience, though being aware of what you dislike is valuable for improving your habits so that you can *be here*. Your awareness of what is happening in the now through your senses will often give you signs as to how you can manifest a better future for yourself, and perhaps even a purpose for your life. You may want to be outside more often, to be in a more active job, or to explore that dream that keeps coming to your mind when you are trying so hard to 'stay on track'. Who knew simply noticing what your body is experiencing in the moment could be so telling? This is why it is always loving to notice the now.

After all is said and done, you get to choose what you make of your time. Through simply doing what you love to do more often, or working on better cultivating your balance so that you can have a future where you will be able to, what you do with your moments will become more purposeful for you. As you begin to understand that time does not get to choose what to make of you, and instead you get to choose what to make of your time, your presence in life will become the greatest present.

Layer Seven: Connecting with Meaning

Layer seven of the High Road invites you to cultivate greater spiritual meaning in your life.

You will gather the strength to move with the currents that come into your life when you open yourself to understanding your spirit. Your spiritual connection will give you the power to let the universe know what you need, and you will feel confident in trusting that it will happen for you.

Rather than living in fear over your sense of purpose, connecting with meaning will allow you to be in alignment with it.

U
Ultimate Calling

Your Ultimate Calling is the purpose of your life. Most of us do not fully see or understand what this purpose is until we grow much older; nonetheless, trusting that we have one allows our desired experiences to enter our lives. When we understand that we are doing what is best for the current phase of our lives, we can enter the active state of 'calling up' what our ultimate calling requires. Eventually, the foundation that you build on the High Road will become a platform, a precipice for that *something greater* that you are meant to become. When we reassure ourselves that the current phase of our lives is essential to our future, any feelings of purposelessness can dissolve.

Phases of Your Calling

You may have experienced times in your life where you felt that meaning was lacking in much that you did. The mountains ahead may have seemed too big to endure climbing, and when walking on your path, your body felt like it was heavy, as though carrying the weight of the world. Perhaps you were only doing the bare minimum, and you might have even wished that you could be anywhere else. The long-term may have made the short-term feel unattainable, as you had not yet realised that meandering along the long-term path enables your deepest fulfilment. In trusting that your ultimate calling is embedded in the very fabric of all layers on your path, the steps will not feel so heavy. You will feel compelled, pulled, and gripped by the journey because you know you are answering the most important calling of all: the calling to become your authentic self.

The voice that speaks loudest to you about what is meaningful and motivating for you ought to be your own. Instead of following what you perceive others want you to do, you could continue exploring what you are passionate about and interested in. You can remind yourself that even the smallest action of doing what you want will connect you directly to the great *why* of your life.

When you notice that you are drifting from choosing curious, intentional actions in your life, or even that the actions that you are choosing feel purposeless, it can help to clarify what your priorities are. Are you making sure that your life is oriented around what you desire to work towards? Without anchoring the current phase of your journey in curiosity, you would likely feel as though you are filling tasks robotically. Although it could appear on the outside that you were making 'progress', choosing to live your life in a way that is not meaningful to you is like listening to a broken record. You can tell yourself that you are progressing when you are spinning forward, but when a vinyl record is scratched it loops, endlessly playing the same segment over and over. The illusion of spinning is that you can appear to be moving, when in reality you need to connect with yourself to move forward in a fulfilled way. The curiosity that your ultimate calling requires of you invites you to heal by imagining what the harmonics of your life could sound like – what are the notes that you want to play, the ones you know that will make your heart sing?

Ask yourself, from a space of love and respect, how

you could make your life purposeful by combining what you are good at and interested in with a sense of beginner's curiosity. Maybe you need to revisit an old project in a new way, or start a new one all together. Give yourself the opportunity to live your life authentically and find fresh perspectives – that is how you manifest your ultimate calling.

Call It Up!

It might sound like an enormous task to live your life in alignment with your ultimate calling. However, you have the capacity to call up whatever you require, and know that it will come, rather than merely *hoping* it will. When you let yourself know that you want to experience an area of life that your heart is calling you towards, simply bringing yourself into this awareness is like calling up the universe. At first, you are going to reach its voicemail machine, as it will take some time for it to answer you. This is the period where you may find yourself just hoping that what you want will come true. Yet from the moment you leave a message in the universe's voicemail, you can *trust* that it will answer you. Because you have chosen to call up what you need in your life as an act of self-love, you deserve to know that the universe is going to receive you. The requests that you make to move towards your ultimate calling, with the well-being of yourself in mind, will always return to your life – just not always in the way that you *think* they will. Still, you will always be amazed by your life when opportunities in your life emerge that make you feel like dreams you did not know you had are coming true.

We tend to carry our cell phones with us wherever we go in case we need to call for help in an emergency. It is as though the universe places an invisible phone in our pocket each morning when we get dressed, so that whenever we need to call for reassurance throughout the day, we can. You can call up the universe when it feels as though you are disconnected from your calling, or like there is something new that you want to begin for the sake of your future. You may even find yourself wanting to meet someone to learn more about a specific interest you have. Although our surroundings can immediately make it seem like nothing is a match to what we feel magnetised to cultivate in our lives, you are always just a call away from having these encounters unfold on your path.

V
Value

What we value in our lives is what we place a high priority on, often based on how worthy or useful we subjectively judge it to be. When we begin to distinguish between what is of value and what is not of value in our lives, we will gain an understanding of what is worth surrounding ourselves with and what we are better off creating distance from. Instead of wrapping ourselves up in other people's ideas as to what we should value, it is life-affirming to decide for ourselves which areas of our lives we care to pour our time and energy into. After all, what we invest in returns to us – it is self-loving to choose wisely.

Valuable Resources

What you hold to a high regard in your life has

already contributed greatly to shaping who you have been so far and who you are going to become. Even if you choose not to value anything, choosing not to create these guidelines is still a choice. At this moment, you may feel like you are not in the 'perfect' environment to thrive, or that the 'perfect' resources you would ideally own are not accessible. Because of these factors, you may mistakenly think that your life has little to no value. However, value comes from the choices that *you* make to place priority on certain areas of your life. It is always a matter of being industrious and resourceful, working with what you currently have.

What resources can you maximise that are already free to you? Any aspect of your life that you can be the driver of represents one of these resources – you can choose to spend them away, or to invest in them by giving them some intentional time and energy. These resources include your ability to surround yourself in specific environments; to surround yourself with those who bring out your best; to dive into learning or immerse yourself in an experience. They include your ability to reflect on what your thoughts, feelings, and actions are signalling to you about your next moves in life; your ability to give and receive love; and your ability to limitlessly dream.

Rather than spending your time searching for something external that could bring value into your life, more often than not, it is better to invest into the value of the present moment. If you are nurturing what has resonated with you from the High Road so far, your motivation is going to be channelled in an energetically healthy way. This will make your life immensely valuable, and it does not cost a cent. Your dedication to balance builds your energy, and your dedication to self-love saves you from wasting any time.

Surrounding Yourself with Higher Value

What you do on a regular basis can be sorted into two categories: one that reflects your surviving, and one that reflects your thriving. What you surround yourself with is what you will become. If you are constantly surrounded by people who do not respect themselves, and lack the willingness to change their patterns, these relationships are likely not of high-value to your life. It may be the case that you need to gently create distance from these relationships, because you know that it is not fair to yourself to be surrounded by unwilling individuals when you are doing your inner work consistently. Remember that you can only change yourself. No one is perfect, though if you are honest with yourself, you can tell which wavelength you are on, and how you are positively impacted by those on similar and dissimilar paths. In higher value relationships, you will bring out the best in people, and people will bring out the best in you. You will not blindly expect others to listen to everything that is happening in your life, but only half-listen to them when they have to speak – you will do everything that you can to be fully present with them. You will love them freely, not only because they have chosen to love you, but because when you look at their character, you feel deeply honoured and blessed to have them in your life. In a high-value relationship, how much you enjoy this person's company is intertwined, in addition to love, with a deep respect for how you see them grow over time.

In low-value relationships, you may need to set 'loving limits' as we discussed in the "Inspire" chapter. Beyond looking to your relationships, it may also be helpful for you to consider the low-value habits in your life that tend to distract you from your potential – what you do *mindfully*, versus what you do *mindlessly*. For example, a low value habit for you might be the hours you spend aimlessly scrolling on social media. Maybe you need to think about using social media intentionally, whether that means moderating who you follow, the notifications you allow, or only keeping the platforms that support your interests and make you feel content to use. The same can be said for watching television – do you more so treat it as a time waster, not really caring about the content you consume? Or, do you watch shows intentionally so that you can explore the areas of life you are curious about?

    The purpose of being more mindful about surrounding yourself with high-value is to make your own decisions about what you care for. Rather than wondering why you are always behind or feeling like you have no energy, being self-aware of what you surround yourself with will give you clues as to how you can create a more sustaining lifestyle. The values that you carry have either been invented by or adopted by you, yet they can be actively refreshed to best suit the calling of your authentic self. Being true to what you value in life is not a matter of cutting out parts of yourself, however. Your experiences with what does not work for you are like the layers necessary to find yourself on higher ground, layers which come to manifestation as a result of positive changes.

W
Withitness

Considering all of the tools that you have gathered to this point, it is largely possible that you have begun to feel that you are *with* your growth and development, rather than *against* it. We invite you to reflect for a moment: do you feel differently from how you did when you first began reading this guide? Perhaps you first experienced disbelief in yourself, or resistance towards all that you were learning was possible for you. If you did, know that this is how we all start our journey – we begin 'within' ourselves, and learn to become 'with' ourselves. You can motivate yourself to continue moving forward by viewing your life from a bird's eye view perspective.

Multidimensional Meaning

In 2000, author and researcher Jay Withgott published an article titled, "Taking a Bird's-Eye View….".

What is revealed in this study can be understood as a valuable metaphor – how birds view their fellow species can teach us how to attune to ourselves and others in a meaningful, enriched way. Withgott writes, "Unlike humans, birds can perceive wavelengths in the ultraviolet as well as the visible range of the spectrum. So a bird is able to see ultraviolet 'colours' in another bird's plumage that humans cannot."[6] In our increasingly modern, fast-paced, and digital lives, most of us probably do not look to the birds very often, let alone think about what their view of life can ground us. Their multidimensional perspective of colour highlights that they view life not just in one dimension, yet so often we can undermine life by viewing it from a limited perspective.

From our ego, we might find ourselves judging others based on the perceptual box that we place them into, which causes us to view ourselves and the people in our lives one-dimensionally. When we solely view people in terms of what we can gain from them, or what they can give to us, we miss the broader "colour spectrum" that encompasses every aspect of their humanity. When we take someone for granted, like one of our parents, for instance, we only think

---

[6] Withgott, Jay. "Taking a Bird's-Eye View...in the UV: Recent studies reveal a surprising new picture of how birds see the world". *Bioscience*, Volume 50 Issue 10, 2000.

about them when we need something. A multidimensional perspective invites us to perceive them for all of their colours and shades, to enable ourselves to find the beauty in all living things.

Sometimes there is too much going on for us to slow down and appreciate ourselves and others. We can practise this perspective when birthdays, thanksgiving, or other holidays arise, taking these opportunities of slowness to vocalise what people have done in past months or years to impact our lives for the better. We can even remind ourselves or others of a certain 'colour' or 'shade' that we value within them – that there is inherent value in people not just because of what they do, but because of who they are within.

From Within to With-it

When you think about the birds flying high over the lands we inhabit, they are able to see that all living things have an essential role to fill. They are able to see the broader scope that the smallest actions have, the ways in which human action and inaction alike impact ourselves and our communities. It is clear that all is interconnected. When you make an excuse or repeat a harmful pattern, the part of yourself that hungers for your gifts aches just as much as the place that you have yet to fill does. The most simple part of it all is that it actually feels better for you to be withit – to allow yourself to go towards your higher calling when you feel its nudge.

Understanding your interconnection with the world from a bird's eye view can allow you to love yourself by being humble. Yes, it is often hard for you, along with every single individual, to remember to walk the High Road. When you acknowledge that it truly is not easy to change sometimes, you can affirm to yourself that you *are* doing hard work, and that is why it is valuable. From this affirmation, you can realise that you are building your self-confidence. You are doing what you objectively know to be right, making strides in your inner world and outer world alike that you once could have only dreamed of! You are changing your life and becoming a better person to be around simultaneously – yet as the "Egolessness" chapter echoes, you are not better than anyone. Living in the spirit of yourself simply means that you are filling a necessary role.

From a bird's eye view, the greater picture suggests that we all have something that we need to move with.

When you remain within your personal, subjective reality all of the time, you might fail to see how this disconnects you from your very own character development. You may even lack the *humility* to do what everyone else is doing, which often comes from a lack of knowledge – do not blame yourself if this has been the case. You now have this knowledge, and can choose to live it on your own journey, or even share it with others. Everyone arrives at withitness in their own time, which is why it is important to be gentle with yourself and others. Affirm to yourself that while the uniqueness of your individual path is important, you want to be interconnected with the world, to be a part of collective thriving through your own insightful journey.

We are always just a part of other people's lives, there for a very specific purpose that is not meant to feed our ego. For instance, when you are at work, you have obligations to fulfil just as everyone else does, yet this does not make you any more or less important. It makes you more capable of accepting reality, and finding meaning within that reality. This acceptance can also help calm your mind when you feel anxious. You can empathise with others when you are not so self-focused, instead remembering how you are a part of the whole. You will respect yourself when you also respect others who are also doing the essential work of their purpose.

    The reality of being human is that we all need to live for a reason, and living for this reason is a full-time commitment that requires the best of us. Withitness represents the reality of the balanced conditions that we need to thrive, yet it also punctuates that only through living this reality can there be any magic. We all do not get to float away on the dreamy clouds of self-indulgence as our cultures, belief systems, and generational influences may have taught us to. But from a bird's eye view, looking out for the harmony of inner and outer life alike, we know that being within does not serve anyone's higher good, anyways. It is a joy to be a working part of the beauty in the world that you see, and in knowing this, you can reassure yourself, *it's not so bad. It turns out I'm on the right path, after all.*

X

X Marks Your Spot

At the place in which you are currently standing on your path, you can breathe life into more that you have kept hidden or unexplored. We are all born with an invisible treasure chest that is carried along with us, holding our 'inner riches' in the form of inborn talents, strengths, and interests. When we notice where X marks the spot on our path, we can occupy ourselves with digging up and uncovering this wealth from within. Throughout this entire journey, the focus has been related to enriching your own inner world so that you feel more loving and balanced in your life in a broader range of external circumstances. Your inner riches relate to all that is beneath the surface within yourself, and the process of embodying this latent potential is exactly what it means to dig up your buried treasure. When you choose to do so, you will find yourself growing into new facets that prove to be abundant and life-affirming, adding value to your life that allows you to feel enlivened by your travels.

Finding X

The first step in the process of retrieving your inner treasure is to notice the difference between which parts of you lack value, and the parts of you that are invaluable. It is like looking at the raw material of yourself and deciding that it is only worthwhile to work with what comes naturally to you, as when it comes to the resources of your strengths, there is a sense of infiniteness. You might experience resistance in your life, for instance, if you are tending to a part of yourself that is not high-value – something that you are not strong at or even interested in as it relates to your dreams. This inner treasure will bend and break as you work harder to nourish it, but your most authentic inner riches grow stronger as you care for them.

Although you constantly have access to the wealth within you, you might only notice your treasures when they gleam in the sunshine of positive circumstances. Oftentimes we have to make the effort to dig them out even in the darkness. The seasons of life fluctuate like a rhythm because we need the shadows to motivate us to do illuminating work. Just as a nocturnal animal uses their ability of night vision, your ability to remember that you already have all that you need is like having an extra sense. Through reminding yourself that X marks the spot where you are currently standing on your path, and that it always will, you give yourself the understanding that all that makes you valuable is not separate from your path. What you love in life does not have to be what you keep to the side. Every single one of your talents and interests can become something worth bringing into your life when you remember that your spirit is willing to work for it.

  Spiritual prosperity, the ultimate root of fulfilment in life, is ever below your feet when you are on the High Road. Although the potential of your current spot may merely appear to be a sheet of dirt on the road, barren and ordinary, or perhaps even a little slippery and muddy, walking on the High Road permits your inner riches to be buried within every single layer that you travel. Where you are currently standing is where you need to realise your potential more often – all that you need to do to notice how wealthy you are within is to be willing to continue cultivating abundance.

You can affirm that you are currently walking away from external cheapness, from what is self-serving rather than soul-enriching, away from what you have outgrown. You are not surrounding yourself with what is easy when you apply any of the tools about life that you have learned in this guide, and in fact, you are already embodying what it means to bring your inner riches out from the surface when you do. You may have tried to fit into lesser versions of yourself in the past, thinking it would make you rich, when in reality you were on a tightrope, struggling to find balance. You have grown the self-awareness to perceive how these lesser versions do not need to be accepted, as your inner riches promise a golden stability. When you trade the toxicity of drifting for the clarity of presence, you reconnect with your authentic treasures.

It is a better occupation for you to focus on prospering from your inner wealth first. Doing so makes it more likely that you are going to find yourself in a state of playfulness, uncovering unexpected dimensions of yourself through discoveries that are *enjoyable* to be around. If you have been aware of your inner riches for some time, yet have not made the effort to dig them up and bring them to life, now you can directly figure out how you can set yourself up from the onset to do so.

You might know that there are varying points in the day where you find yourself faced with a negative mindset, feeling worthless or drained. In these instances, you could do something to calm and ground your spirit, bringing stillness into your life again. You could return to the chapter on "Affirmations", or "The Time Is Now… Breathe", by reminding yourself that there is a higher path – that your time and energy are to be treated with kindness and gentle purpose. If you make the extra two, five, fifteen, or even thirty minutes to correctly assess and act on how you can remain on a higher path, you are going to feel enriched. From cultivating this richness within, and knowing the humble work that is required to do so, you will have set yourself up to uncover treasure – X marks your spot.

Materialising the Treasure Within

Once you have excavated one of your treasures within, you do not have to rush to materialise it. You see, your inner riches, when you are open to them, are here to teach you as they come to fruition. That is a part of the gold that they represent – they are not going to allow you to settle for less of yourself if you are not going to allow this either. How you can breathe life into them at best is by working with what you uncover with slowness. Slowness can take the form of being quietly gentle with yourself as you go, and treating mistakes as kindred learning opportunities. If you move quickly, your journey might be tainted by your want of reaching an end point, and you will find yourself staring yet again at the ground, feeling that it is just the boring floor of earth.

    With slowness comes the fact that you need to choose not to avoid doing the work, though rather to figure out how you can be at one with the work. Your inner wealth will begin to rust or erode if you set it aside on the High Road, and it may even do this if you do not show up consistently. If enough time passes, it will slowly become buried back under, and, well... you will patiently have to begin again. This regression can be avoided by thinking in terms of *now*. X is the higher place between stagnation and rushing where the inner wealth you have chosen to work with will thrive. Although no one can take what you have chosen from you, because it is entirely yours, you can take it away from yourself if you are not slowing down to be consistent.

Knowing that you will prosper both spiritually and materially from the treasure within you, it is self-loving to challenge yourself to regularly make the time to connect with it in your life – at least every week, if not even for a window of time each day. The more often that you make the time to connect with your inner riches, the more you can trust that your potential will come to fruition rather than fade. How could it not when you are giving the best of you?

Even though it will feel uncomfortable in the beginning, encourage yourself to be brave, to follow your momentum without setting any limits. You know that the only limits you set stem from your own perception, though now that your eyes are on solid gold, this is what you can focus on instead. Once you have discovered one of your treasures, and have given yourself permission to be present with it until it develops into a passion, there is nothing that could hold you back except for self-imposed limits. Yet these are the same limits that held you back from digging to begin with, and you have already passed that point. Rather than accepting less of ourselves when we are tempted not to be with our inner treasures, we can reassure ourselves that we would like to look back on our lives and say that we did not allow for any of the potential within ourselves to fade away. The excuses that we make not to connect with our buried treasure and live it out in our lives do come at a detrimental cost.

You are here, and there are decisions to make. Yet the amazing news is that bringing yourself into the awareness that you need to find X can help you to awaken to what is truly gold within you. What is truly gold within you is the person that you are at your best, who you become when you choose to be interested in what you see flickering within, needing to expand. When you let yourself know that your fear towards this new potential is also your excitement, not only will X mark your spot where you are standing, but it will also become a string of uncovered opportunities. These opportunities will exist behind and ahead of you, acting as markers of what has already been great and what could become even better. Through being connected to your current place in life, a series of future places will begin to open for you. These future places carry the experiences that you need to fully give yourself the unconditional love for life that you deserve to have. It is time for you to love yourself by uncovering one of your inner riches, mastering it, and then digging up the next. X marks your spot!

Layer Eight: (Un)ending

Although conclusions signify the end of a book, this book can continue to be an active guide for you as you build your foundation. The journey is the end point, after all.

If you ever find yourself falling out of alignment, this layer is here to remind you as to how you can return to the High Road for guidance.

Choosing more of your potential, rather than less, will become your consistent lifestyle. In always remembering your intentions, you will come to feel at one with your life, and remain in a state of constant growth through loving yourself, your balance, and your life.

Y
Yes to Life

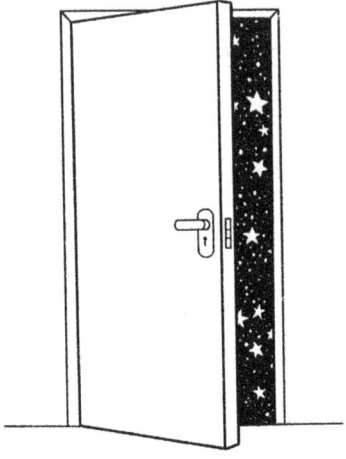

Whether we say yes or no to life is the decision we make when we have one foot in an open door, so to speak. Maybe we have just made the effort to dig up one of our inner riches, and find ourselves in an unknown situation where we are unsure as to whether we are capable of, deserving of, or even willing to move forward. In this unsteady place, it is important for us to empathise with ourselves about how we are feeling, and continue to feel our way through it to a positive affirmation – *when I say yes to life more often, more will happen in my life!* You deserve to accept more of yourself, to walk through the open doors that you bravely and mindfully choose.

Mindfully Welcoming the Unknown

Saying yes can only result in positive changes when you are either intentionally choosing the doors you would like to walk through, or aware of when an offering has potential. Still, the moment before making the decision to welcome the unknown can generate thoughts of fear. It is easier to follow this fear and say no than it is to say yes, but when we say no, we create distrust within ourselves. We can continue to build trust within by affirming that when we say yes to life, *we are not going to lose anything*. Rather than losing, we are going to prosper and thrive.

The root of yes, when said with mindful intentions, is trust. The tricky part is that you may find yourself excitedly tripping over this root when a new door awaits you, which causes you to change your mind and say no out of fear. When you neglect yourself from walking through the doors that you have already thought your way towards (perhaps you had even begun twisting open the door handle, peering to look at the new scenery on the other side), there can be a sense of disbelief. Yes, it can feel impossible to surrender to the unknown, even when you know it is going to be better for you. But without a doubt, when you have thought and felt your way towards the best opportunities, they are yours to own.

When you shift into yes-mode, you are loving yourself and your life. The odds become much more likely that you are going to create valuable memories, or learn the lessons that are required for you to have a thorough understanding of yourself. These are much better options compared to remaining in the stagnation that blankets you when you say no. Remember our discussion on failing forward in "Faith in Yourself"? When you choose to accept more of who you are and what you would like to experience in life, the unknown will show you parts of yourself that you would not have been able to discover in denial. Over time, as you follow through on being genuinely open with yourself, you will contribute to a pattern. You will realise that you would not have been able to create any of those chapters, learn any of those lessons, or develop the strong character that you now have without accepting the offerings that came your way.

You may already be saying yes to life more than you know. Your path on the High Road has been an adventure of receiving, opening yourself to, and developing what you had a feeling was there within you. To fully gather the tools that you needed, you needed to welcome each chapter like you were saying yes to a new day! How is this for an affirmation – *I have already welcomed the unknown into my life, and have positively benefited from it. There is only more for me now.*

Continuing to practise self-awareness involves knowing when you would actually benefit from moving through a door, even though you may be afraid or insecure. If you know the external circumstance that causes you to say no, or potentially to even self-sabotage, then you know saying yes is the tool you need to drive towards life-affirming affirmations. Yes – your mindfully chosen, new experiences *will* generate healing and learning.

To say yes to life, it is important to be open to receiving invitations – the only person who will stop you from doing so is yourself, just as you are the only person who can allow yourself to say yes to begin with. Whether in your work life, family life, or social life, the only way that you are going to know when you are being given the opportunity to say yes, and to say it, is through trusting yourself first. When you feel your inner riches calling to you, instead of putting them aside, you could say yes to life by giving them five minutes of your time before falling asleep. There are all of these windows of distraction that you can glance at briefly, though there is only one door that is going to take you out of the infrastructure that you have boxed yourself into. You can choose to head to the door, giving yourself the freedom to venture out and find the next X of inner riches at your feet.

Really, every letter in this A-Z guide has been a tool, but you also might consider it to be a door. Each time that you sense it is time to apply what has resonated with you, you will have to continue feeling towards the power of your own affirmation. When an opportunity for self-growth arises, you can train yourself to see beyond your wavering fear – that, *yes!* – you have found a door. You can reassure yourself, *I may not know entirely what lies beyond it, but I trust that I am safe. I feel this is right for me, and although I may walk imperfectly, it is more loving to make the effort than it is to stay inside.*

Z
Zeroes Are No Longer Permitted

We have briefly spoken about the importance of gratitude in this guide, and we would like to take this chapter to thank you. Thank you for trusting yourself to learn more about your individual growth, and for trusting us as your guides. It is easy knowledge that trust is built over time, though understanding and applying it to our lives is often a difficult task. So why do it? Because it is worth it. *You* are worth it. Moving forward, self-love will always be a choice, an optional practice for you. No one is ever going to force you to do it, because it is the natural calling within you that only you can rise with. We invite you to end where you began: with an affirmation. We invite you to gently let yourself know that zeroes are no longer permitted for you.

From Dawn to Dusk

The moments while reading this guide that caused you to reassess your life are more valuable than any of the words we have written. Your voice and self-connection are what you awake with and live with everyday. From dawn to dusk, you will always be in conversation with yourself, and it will always be up to you to continue this conversation gently. You are worth knowing. Now that you are aware that you are being guided in this life, you know that anytime you need further support, you can have it. The desires of your higher calling make it so that you are hardwired to fulfil yourself – therefore, zeroes are no longer permitted.

Every day, you have the choice to build upwards. You know that each time you do this, you add a layer, an amendment to what was empty before. It is only human for there to be times where you want to turn back, though do you really believe you will ever stop wanting more for yourself out of self-love? Now that you have brought yourself into greater awareness, you are on the path that you knew you needed to land on. You chose this guide because you listened to *yourself*. The journey has already taken you this far, and now that you are on the path you wanted to be on, you do not have to turn back. The mountains have been ground down to molehills; the roadblocks have replaced themselves with speed bumps; the pitfalls and dark caves do not look as inviting as they once did. The simple ways to thrive that you observed were already prominent within you. From time to time, you may just need a reminder that you are not worth forgetting about.

You have chosen to understand and believe in the higher good of yourself, and how you can attract more of what you need in your life by doing your inner work. You now know that when you make a difference within yourself, even when you feel at your lowest, positive changes are nothing short of small miracles that will appear in your life many times over.

Making changes within yourself allows you to come together with others and make changes in the world. Self-improvement can sound too tedious or overwhelming of a task, which is why many often turn away. Yet the tools you have found meaningful from this guide seem so simple at times because they are an echo of what is already present within you. If you find yourself feeling fearful before walking the High Road, you can trust this is actually a good sign. Your fear will transform into life-affirming feelings as you continue following through on what you know is best.

Thank you for being who you are as an individual. Thank you for opening yourself up to improving your life, and making inputs towards cultivating greater self-love and balance. You now know that with the most simple effort, you will always find yourself on the path of least resistance – living life one letter at a time. We believe that when we strengthen ourselves, we strengthen our humanity – our ability to empathise with, connect with, and share with others. At a time where so many of us have become isolated, or feel like we have lost sight of what is most important in our lives, finding the High Road creates healing on the individual and universal level.

When we self-accept, we can accept reality for what it is. When we choose mindful actions, we will not question whether we are going in the right direction. When we are open to possibility, we will be able to move away from the crowd and create our own fulfilment. When we perceive life differently, the negativity we experience will dissolve. When we engage with life differently, we will find ourselves immersed in experiences that calm us, that draw out all of our inborn potential. When we enhance our mindfulness, we will come to know and love ourselves better. When we connect with meaning, we will feel a deep peace in knowing our place in this world, and when we remind ourselves the journey is unending, we will be able to return to this guide whenever we are ready to start anew.

We invite you to allow this ending to be your beginning, and to express gratitude to yourself for walking the High Road.

Acknowledgements

Terry would like to thank his wife Andrea, his daughter Kayla, his brothers Timothy and Jason, his father Desmond, and most especially his mother Marthe, his greatest inspiration. Jillian-Rae would like to thank her mother Geraldine, her father Raymond, her sister Maggie, and her family in Newfoundland. We are both grateful for your unconditional love – thank you for always believing in us.

We are most thankful to Abbey Laferriere, our dear friend and respected colleague. She created the stunning cover and chapter designs for this book, and remained our steady editing guide from beginning to end. We would also like to thank our dear friend and colleague Tony Cox, who is a constant inspiration in our lives. We are thankful to Francesco Tignanelli, and graduates of the S.O.L.E. Program – Julia Minor, Elizabeth Szaranski, Samuel Kostopoulos, and Chloe Carriere – whose feedback was crucial to the editing process. Thank you to Tory Fisher, Renee Lacoursiere, Lianne Van De Wal, Katherine Zappala and Les Gorman for supporting our creative journey throughout the years. Lastly, thank you to past and present S.O.L.E. crews – you are always in our hearts.

References

Henry David Thoreau, *Walden* (University of Virginia, 1888), p.55.

Jay Withgott, "Taking a Bird's-Eye View...in the UV: Recent studies reveal a surprising new picture of how birds see the world" (*Bioscience,* Volume 50, Issue 10, 2000), p.854-859.

Lesley Lyle, *Laugh Your Way to Happiness* (Watkins Media, 2014), p.15.

Mark Anthony Jacobson, *Ojibway Clans: Animal Totems and Spirits* (Native Northwest, 2015), p.1-23.

Steve Van Matre and Bill Weiler, *The Earth Speaks* (Institute for Earth Education), p.3.

Wayne Dyer, *The Power of Intention* (Hay House, 2006), p.154.

If you enjoyed *The Insightful Journey*, we invite you to read our other book in the growing collection of the *Walking the High Road* series.

Whether you're looking to better ground yourself in the present moment, remind yourself of the fabric through which your contentment is crafted, or simply take a long, deep breath of fresh air – *Canoeing with the Seasons* has something to offer you that will make a lasting positive impact.

Available at www.enablingpotential.ca

Made in the USA
Monee, IL
03 May 2026

49438365R00115